VOGUE
AUSTRALIA
COOK
BOOK

VOGUE AUSTRALIA COOK BOOK

Compiled by

Sheila Scotter and Elizabeth Reeve

NELSON

THOMAS NELSON (AUSTRALIA) LTD
597 Little Collins Street Melbourne 3000
403 George Street Sydney 2000

THOMAS NELSON AND SONS LTD
36 Park Street London W1Y 4DE

THOMAS NELSON AND SONS (SOUTH AFRICA) PTY LTD
P.O. Box 9881 Johannesburg

THOMAS NELSON AND SONS (CANADA) LTD
81 Curlew Drive Don Mills Ontario

Cover design by Warren Scott
Drawings by Sally Doust
Designed by Michael Smith, M.S.I.A.
Printed in Hong Kong
by Dai Nippon Printing Co. (International) Ltd

Contents

❧❀❧

Winning Starters

COLD PLUM SOUP

MOCK MULLIGATAWNY

AVGOLEMONO

GREEN GAZPACHO

PÂTÉ MAISON

EGG STARTER

OEUFS EN COCOTTE

CURRIED EGG MOUSSE

PRAWNS MARINIÈRE

HAWAIIAN CRAB

SCALLOP COCKTAIL

SMOKED SALMON AND AVOCADO CREAM

MOULES À LA POULETTE

HOT GRAPEFRUIT

RATATOUILLE WITH FENNEL

CUCUMBER AND YOGHURT SALAD

ORANGE AND MINT SALAD

RICE AND PEAS SALAD

WATERCRESS AND MUSHROOM SALAD

ABRUZZI SALAD

THE FIRST COURSE for a family meal or dinner party can be as simple as avocado, leeks or artichoke hearts *vinaigrette*, as rich as goose liver pâté or as wholesome and non-calorific as a vegetable salad. It can have the bland smoothness of a mousse, or the tang of seafood, depending on the courses that follow and the balance of the complete meal. Because starters which can be prepared ahead and go straight from refrigerator to table are convenient for the busy hostess, most of the following recipes are served cold.

COLD PLUM SOUP

⊷⊱❋⊰⊶

2 pounds red plums
6 cups chicken stock
2 tablespoons fine tapioca
2 cups Sauterne-type white wine
¼ cup granulated sugar
3 cloves

1 lemon, sliced paper-thin and seeded
¾ cup toasted slivered almonds
Salt, cayenne
Dash of nutmeg

Bring 2 cups chicken stock to the boil and trickle in tapioca, stirring to prevent sticking. Simmer until transparent. In another pan, combine washed and stemmed plums, the rest of the stock, wine, sugar, cloves and lemon. Simmer for 10 to 15 minutes or until plums are tender. Remove plums, cut in halves and discard stones. Return plum halves to mixture and season with a little salt, cayenne and nutmeg. Combine with tapioca and stock mixture. Chill for several hours. Serve in chilled cups, sprinkled with almonds.

MOCK MULLIGATAWNY

⊷⊱❋⊰⊶

1 16-ounce can pea soup
1 16-ounce can cream of tomato soup
2 cans water

2 cans milk
Curry powder or paste, to taste
¼ pint cream

Combine soups in a heavy saucepan, and dilute first with water (use the can as a measure), then add milk. Add curry to taste, heat to boiling point. Remove from heat, add cream and serve.

AVGOLEMONO

⊷⊱❋⊰⊶

3 cups rich chicken stock
½ cup washed long-grain rice
Salt

2 whole eggs
2 egg yolks
Juice of 2 lemons

Bring chicken stock to boil and add rice. Cook until tender. Salt, if necessary. Beat eggs and egg yolks until light and frothy and add the lemon juice slowly, beating it in. Add a little of the hot stock to the egg mixture, blending it in well and slowly add this to the rest of the stock, stirring constantly. Heat through, but do not boil. Serves 6.

GREEN GAZPACHO

❦❉❦

1 clove garlic
2 slices white bread with crusts
   removed
¼ cup Spanish olive oil
6 to 8 medium green tomatoes
1 green pepper
1 cucumber

1 tablespoon onion, grated
½ teaspoon salt
2 tablespoons vinegar
Good pinch of cumin
½ to ¾ cup ice water
½ to ¾ cup dry white wine

GARNISHES: *chopped red tomato, unpeeled cucumber and onion, minced hard-boiled egg, crisp, fried croûtons*

Put garlic through garlic press, add bread and cover with olive oil. Leave for several hours or overnight. Scald tomatoes with boiling water, peel and cut into quarters. Seed and chop green pepper, peel and dice cucumber and onion, combine with tomatoes and purée in electric blender a little at a time, or put through a mincer. Combine oil-soaked bread, salt, vinegar and cumin. Add half this mixture at a time to purée in blender (or electric mixer) and beat until very smooth. Chill thoroughly. Just before serving, blend in ice water and wine until soup is desired consistency.

PÂTÉ MAISON

❦❉❦

½ pound bacon
¼ cup brandy
1½ pounds each beef and calves'
   liver, minced
½ pound pork liver, minced

2 eggs
¼ cup sour cream
Salt, black pepper, a little
   crushed garlic
3 or 4 chicken livers

Line a pâté mould with thinly sliced, rindless bacon; sprinkle with a little brandy. Mix minced livers with eggs, sour cream and seasonings. Pour on remaining brandy, flaming. Mix well and half-fill mould with mixture. Put chicken livers in a row down the centre. Cover with rest of pâté; then top with bacon. Cover with foil, stand mould in pan of water and bake (300°F.) for about 2 hours. Remove and cool. Put brick on top to press down firmly and chill for 24 hours. Turn out and cut as many slices as required. Arrange on a platter in overlapping slices and surround with chopped aspic.

EGG STARTER

❧❀❧

8 hard-boiled eggs	½ cup good mayonnaise
½ cup cream	1 16-ounce can beef consommé

Halve the eggs lengthwise and arrange, cut side down, side by side in a shallow serving dish. In a bowl beat together cream, mayonnaise and ½ cup of consommé which has been chilled in the can but not allowed to jelly. When well blended, pour mixture over eggs. Place dish immediately in refrigerator. After sauce has set around the eggs (this takes several hours, or they could be left in refrigerator overnight), carefully spoon chilled consommé remaining in can all over the top, like a glaze. Return to refrigerator to set. Serve with slices of French bread. Serves 6 to 8.

OEUFS EN COCOTTE

❧❀❧

¼ pound mushrooms	6 eggs
¼ pint cream	Salt and pepper
1 tablespoon finely-chopped parsley	Sherry or Sauterne-type wine

GARNISH: *grated cheese and watercress*

Place 12 peeled whole mushrooms in a buttered pan. Sprinkle with salt, cook in oven 5 minutes. Set aside. Mix strips of uncooked mushrooms with cream and add parsley. Warm and butter 6 individual ramekins, divide raw mushroom mixture between them, break a whole egg into each and season with salt and pepper. Mix a little more cream with a good tablespoon of the wine and pour some of this over each dish. Bake until eggs are set, then top each with 2 cooked mushrooms and place under a hot grill for a few minutes. Grate a little cheese on top and garnish with watercress. Serves 6.

CURRIED EGG MOUSSE

(Mrs Carey Younghusband)

❧❀❧

12 hard-boiled eggs	1 tablespoon curry powder
¾ pint cream	Paprika
1 tablespoon gelatine	Salt and pepper

GARNISH: *prawns and sliced cucumber*

Chop or mince eggs finely. Whip cream lightly and gently fold in gelatine and curry powder. Season to taste. Spoon into ring mould and chill until set. To serve, unmould and fill centre with prawns. Top with finely-sliced cucumber. Serves 8.

PRAWNS MARINIÈRE

❧✿❧

2 pounds prawns, shelled and
   cleaned
2 cups white wine
2 cups chicken stock
Bouquet garni (parsley, bayleaf
   and thyme)
⅓ cup green onions, minced

4 tablespoons butter or olive oil
3 tablespoons flour
Salt and pepper, to taste
½ cup cream
3 egg yolks
12 slices French bread, toasted
Finely-chopped parsley

Cook prawns in wine and stock with *bouquet garni* for 5 minutes. Sauté shallots
or green onion in butter or oil. Add flour, cook for a minute or two, then add
to prawn mixture (removing *bouquet garni* as you do so). When smooth and
thickened, add salt and pepper. Cook gently for 10 minutes and, just before
serving, add cream mixed with egg yolks. Do not allow to boil. Serve prawns
in shallow bowl, surrounded with toasted French bread. Sprinkle with
chopped parsley.

HAWAIIAN CRAB

❧✿❧

2 egg yolks
Salt and cayenne, to taste
2 tablespoons tarragon vinegar
1 cup vegetable oil
1 teaspoon Tabasco sauce
2 teaspoons Worcestershire sauce
½ teaspoon sugar
½ cup cream, whipped
½ pound crab meat

1 green pepper, finely chopped
1 red pepper, finely chopped
4 tomatoes, skinned, seeded and
   chopped
½ cup onion, finely chopped
4 small avocado pears
½ pound bacon, slightly grilled
1 teaspoon each garlic and
   parsley, both finely chopped

First, make a spicy mayonnaise; put in a bowl egg yolks, salt, cayenne and
vinegar. Beat well. Slowly beat in oil, Tabasco and Worcestershire sauces and
sugar. Then add whipped cream, crab meat and all other ingredients except
avocado pears and bacon. Divide mixture into buttered, individual
ramekins; arrange peeled, sliced avocados on top. Cover with rashers of
bacon and bake in the oven (375°F.) for 25 minutes. Serve hot. This may be
made as a main course, if baked in one dish.

SCALLOP COCKTAIL

❖❖❖

3 tablespoons white wine
3 tablespoons white wine
  vinegar
1 leek, chopped
1 onion, chopped
1 carrot, chopped
Bouquet garni
Salt and pepper

1 quart cold water
12 to 18 scallops
1 teaspoon mustard
1 teaspoon vinegar
½ pint cream
1 heaped teaspoon paprika
1 tablespoon Italian vermouth
Cayenne

Make a *court bouillon* with white wine, vinegar, vegetables, *bouquet garni*; salt, pepper and water. Simmer until vegetables are cooked. Strain off liquid, and in it poach opened scallops for 5 minutes. Drain, chop roughly, mix white flesh and coral and divide between 6 or 8 serving glasses. Mix in a bowl 1 teaspoon each of mustard and vinegar; season with salt and pepper. Gradually stir in cream, then paprika and vermouth. Add dash of cayenne if desired. Pour over scallops, and serve very cold. Serves 6 to 8.

SMOKED SALMON AND AVOCADO CREAM

❖❖❖

½ pound smoked salmon
2 avocado pears
Lemon juice

Freshly-ground black pepper
Cayenne

Mince, or finely chop, salmon. Halve avocados lengthwise, discard stones, then scoop out flesh, leaving skins intact. Mash flesh thoroughly with lemon juice, then mix with salmon. Dust with black and cayenne pepper. Pile back into avocado skins; chill. Serves 4.

MOULES À LA POULETTE

❖❖❖

1 onion, finely chopped
2 ounces butter
Chopped parsley
Freshly-ground black pepper

1 bottle dry white wine
1 gallon scrubbed mussels
2 egg yolks
½ pint cream

Using a large enamel pan, sauté onion in butter for 5 minutes until transparent. Add parsley, pepper and wine. As soon as wine begins to boil, tip in half the mussels. Cover pan, shake once or twice, and steam mussels for 4 to 5 minutes. When they start to open (as they do), pick out with perforated spoon and place in covered dish to keep warm. Repeat process with remaining mussels. Reduce cooking liquid by fast boiling. Add salt if needed. Take off heat, and thicken liquid with egg yolks beaten into cream. Be careful not to have pan too hot or this will curdle. Correct seasoning, pour the sauce over mussels and serve immediately.

HOT GRAPEFRUIT

(Mrs John Somerset)

❧❀❧

Grapefruit

Sugar

Dry sherry

Maraschino cherries

Allow half a grapefruit for each serving. Remove pips and cut sections in usual way, sprinkle with a teaspoon of sugar, then put under a medium griller until well-heated. Just before serving, sprinkle one dessertspoon of medium dry sherry over each half and decorate with a maraschino cherry.

RATATOUILLE WITH FENNEL

❧❀❧

2 large onions, sliced

3 (or more) cloves of garlic, chopped

⅓ cup olive oil

2 small eggplants, cubed

4 small zucchini, sliced

2 green peppers, cut in strips

1 head fennel, sliced

1 pound plum tomatoes

1 teaspoon basil

1½ teaspoons salt

½ teaspoon parsley

Freshly-ground black pepper to taste

Sauté onions and garlic in a skillet with oil, tossing until wilted. Add egg-plant, zucchini, peppers and fennel. Mix well over brisk heat. Add tomatoes and seasonings. Cover and simmer about 1 hour, stirring occasionally. Remove cover and allow to reduce until most of the liquid has evaporated and mixture is thick. Serve hot or cold. Serves 6.

CUCUMBER AND YOGHURT SALAD

❧❀❧

4 cucumbers

1½ teaspoons salt

1 clove garlic, minced

2 tablespoons lemon juice

2 cups yoghurt

1 tablespoon dill, chopped

¼ cup olive oil

2 teaspoons fresh mint, chopped

Peel cucumbers, cut in quarters lengthwise, then slice thinly and sprinkle with salt. Drain well. Mix garlic, lemon juice, yoghurt and dill, then mix with cucumbers. Pour oil over top, sprinkle with mint. Serve unchilled. Serves 8.

ORANGE AND MINT SALAD

Oranges
Mint, finely chopped
¼ cup olive oil

1 tablespoon lemon juice
1 tablespoon Cognac

Peel oranges, removing all white pith. Slice, discarding ends, and arrange in overlapping slices on plates. Sprinkle with chopped fresh mint. Make a dressing by combining remaining ingredients, pour over slices and chill well. Serve without lettuce. Watercress may be added as a garnish.

RICE AND PEAS SALAD

1½ cups long-grain rice
½ cup French dressing

1 packet frozen peas, cooked
2-ounce can pimiento

Bring 2 quarts water to a rolling boil. Add rice slowly and cook for 14 minutes or until tender but still firm. Drain well; add dressing and peas. Drain pimiento, cut into strips, saving all scraps. Mince scraps, fold into rice, pack into a bowl and chill. At serving time, unmould on to a platter and arrange pimiento strips over the dome of rice. Serves 8.

WATERCRESS AND MUSHROOM SALAD

2 cups watercress, washed
2 cups mushrooms, sliced

¾ cup radishes, sliced
⅓ cup French dressing

Arrange watercress in centre of bowl. Cover with mushrooms and radishes, mixed together. Pour dressing over. Serves 6.

ABRUZZI SALAD

In a bowl, combine thinly-sliced oranges (with rind) and Italian or Greek black olives. Add a small amount of olive oil and toss lightly.

2

Recipes for Busy People

QUICK SPINACH SOUP

ICED TURTLE SOUP

SMOKED OYSTER SOUP

POLISH-STYLE BAKED FISH

PAN-FRIED TROUT

PRAWNS AND MUSHROOMS

MARROW SOUFFLÉ

CHEESE SOUFFLÉ

QUICK SOUFFLÉ

MUSHROOM SOUFFLÉ

SPAGHETTI ALL' CARBONARA

CHICKEN À LA KING

CHICKEN AND HAM CASSEROLE

QUICK CHICKEN CASSEROLE

CHICKEN NAPOLITAINE

QUICK LUNCHEON DISH

MOUSSAKA

ANYTHING MARENGO

FILLET OF BEEF

PORK AND APPLE PIE

ONIONS MONÉGASQUE

PARTY SPROUTS

MOCK WILD RICE

ANYTHING-GOES PURÉE

WE HAVE DEDICATED this chapter to the cook who is pressed for time but refuses to settle for a steady diet of quick grills. In it are ideas for easy-to-make soups and main dishes; several of them contributed by Australian women who have demanding careers yet are able to produce delicious, interesting meals when they entertain mid-week. Some recipes are prepared the night before and reheated; others use frozen or canned foods, imaginatively treated. Soufflés are included too, because once you have mastered the knack of making them, they can be prepared in minutes and don't take long in the oven. Many recipes for easy-to-make puddings are included in the chapter 'Desserts with a Difference', starting on page 103.

QUICK SPINACH SOUP

❧❀❧

1 packet frozen leaf spinach
Chicken stock
1 large onion, chopped
Salt and pepper

Approximately 1½ tablespoons
   butter
¼ pint cream
1 egg yolk

In a large saucepan, sauté 1 chopped onion (or 2 small onions) in butter until soft. Add frozen spinach from packet and allow it to thaw. Add almost ½ pint chicken stock (which may be made from cubes) and place in blender—blend at speed 2 for 30 seconds, then at speed 4 for 30 seconds. Add salt to taste and freshly-ground pepper. Return to pan and simmer. Before serving, add cream and egg yolk; do not let boil. Serve with *croûtons*, or with buttered toast fingers of Vogel brown bread for luncheon. (For a quick, spur-of-the-moment lunch, follow with assorted cheeses, then coffee and ginger chocolates.)

ICED TURTLE SOUP

(Mrs Philip Jacobsen)

❧❀❧

1 ounce gelatine
1 16-ounce can clear turtle soup
¾ can water
Dry sherry

Lemon juice
Sour cream
Caviar

Dissolve gelatine in water and mix with turtle soup. Using the empty can as a measure, fill it with ¾ can water and then fill to the top with equal quantities of dry sherry and lemon juice. No seasoning is needed. Chill in a bowl in refrigerator. Spoon into serving cups; top each with a dollop of sour cream (about 1 dessertspoon) and sprinkle caviar on top. Do not garnish until ready to serve. This can be made either the night before or the morning of the day it is required.

SMOKED OYSTER SOUP

❧❀❧

1 16-ounce can smoked oysters | Salt and pepper
1 16-ounce can oyster soup | ¼ pint cream
1 soup-can of milk | 1 dessertspoon dry sherry

This soup takes only minutes to prepare, and is served hot. Coarsely chop the oysters and put them, with the contents of the soup-can, in a saucepan. Using the can as a measure, add 1 can of milk. Season to taste and heat slowly, so that the flavour of the smoked oysters permeates the soup, but do not let boil. Remove from heat, stir in cream and sherry, and serve. Serves 4.

POLISH-STYLE BAKED FISH

❧❀❧

Olive oil | 4 frozen fish fillets
Fresh breadcrumbs | Fresh dill, chopped
1 large onion | Sour cream
1 tablespoon butter | Finely-chopped parsley

Brush a loaf tin with olive oil and sprinkle thickly with fresh breadcrumbs. Sauté onion, sliced paper-thin, in butter until crisp and brown. Drain. Put layers of fish fillets alternately with onion slices, chopped dill and a thick layer of sour cream, making four layers in all. Cover well with sour cream; bake in moderate oven (400°F.) 25 to 30 minutes or until fish flakes easily when tested with a fork. Garnish with parsley. Serves 4.

PAN-FRIED TROUT

❧❀❧

Frozen rainbow trout | Flour
Mustard | Bacon fat
Salt and pepper | 1 clove of garlic

Defrost trout. Rub outside with dry mustard, sprinkle salt and pepper inside. Shake in paper bag with flour. Fry in fresh bacon fat, with crushed garlic. Serve, garnished with bacon rashers.

PRAWNS AND MUSHROOMS

⊰✤⊱

4 cups cooked prawns
3 cups mushrooms
½ cup stuffed olives

1 cup small boiled onions
Béchamel sauce
Grated cheese

Put peeled, cleaned prawns in a pan with mushrooms, olives and onions. Cover with béchamel sauce made with a little dry mustard. Sprinkle with grated cheese and bake until golden.

SOUFFLÉS
Basic method

A soufflé is only a white sauce enriched with yolks and lightened by beaten egg whites. For a result which will be perfect every time, follow these rules meticulously:

1 Bowl and whisk must be clean and dry.
2 When separating eggs, take care not to let a speck of yolk into the whites.
3 Do not overbeat the whites: they should be just stiff enough to stand in creamy peaks when the whisk is held upright.
4 Fold in whites immediately they reach right consistency, otherwise they will become watery.
5 Work with the utmost speed and serve straight from the oven to the table. Soufflés won't wait!

MARROW SOUFFLÉ
(Mrs G. F. de Gruchy)

⊰✤⊱

1 pound small marrows
  (2- to 8-inches long)
1 ounce butter
2 tablespoons flour
¼ pint warm milk

Salt and pepper
5 tablespoons Gruyère cheese,
  grated
2 egg yolks
4 egg whites

Slice unpeeled marrows (pare rough edges off larger ones); salt and leave to drain. Then cook in heavy saucepan with a ladle of water until quite soft and liquid has evaporated. (Add more water if they dry up, but it is important to use as little water as possible.) Sieve, and stir puréed marrows into a béchamel sauce made from butter, flour, milk and seasonings. Add cheese, remove from heat, then add 2 well-beaten egg yolks. Cool, then gently fold in the stiffly beaten whites. Pour into soufflé dish and stand in baking tin of water. Cook in preheated oven (350°F.) for about 23 minutes, until well-risen but still creamy in the centre. Serves 6.

CHEESE SOUFFLÉ

❧❀❧

4 tablespoons melted butter
4 tablespoons flour
1 cup milk
1 teaspoon dry mustard

½ teaspoon French mustard
1 cup Gruyère cheese, grated
1 cup Parmesan cheese, grated
6 eggs

Melt butter and blend in flour. Bring to boil and add to *roux*. Cook, stirring constantly, until flour is cooked and sauce is smooth. Add the mustards. Remove from heat; stir in cheese and cool slightly. Separate yolks and whites of eggs, then add lightly beaten egg yolks to sauce. Beat egg whites until stiff and fold gently into mixture. Pour into greased soufflé dish. Stand in shallow pan of water and bake in a preheated oven (375°F.) for 45 to 50 minutes. Serve immediately.

QUICK SOUFFLÉ

❧❀❧

3 eggs
1 can mushroom *or* chicken soup
7-ounce can tuna *or* 1 cup
   minced ham
½ cup whole kernel corn or green peas

1 tablespoon cheese, grated
Pinch of basil
Salt and pepper
1 tablespoon dry sherry

Separate yolks and whites of eggs. Beat egg whites until stiff. Beat yolks until lemon-coloured. Stir yolks into soup. Add tuna or ham, corn or peas, cheese, basil, seasonings and sherry. Mix well. Fold in whites. Pour into greased soufflé dish. Put into preheated oven (400°F.) and reduce heat to 350°F. Bake 1 hour and serve immediately.

MUSHROOM SOUFFLÉ

❧❀❧

2 level tablespoons chicken or
   bacon fat
3 tablespoons flour
½ teaspoon salt
Pinch of cayenne
¾ cup milk

½ cup sautéed mushrooms, sliced
3 or 4 egg yolks
2 tablespoons Parmesan cheese,
   grated
5 egg whites

Melt fat, remove from heat and stir in flour, salt and cayenne pepper. When well blended, add milk gradually and stir over heat until mixture thickens. Add mushrooms, egg yolks and cheese. Fold in stiffly beaten egg whites. Grease an 8-inch soufflé dish and tie a band of wax paper round the outside. Pour in mixture and bake for 30 minutes (400°F.). Serves 4.

SPAGHETTI ALL'CARBONARA

(Miss Luciana Arrighi)

❧❀❧

1 pound spaghetti
4 tablespoons olive oil
5 or 6 rashers bacon

2 cloves garlic
6 tablespoons thick cream
1 raw egg

Cook spaghetti in boiling salted water; drain and mix with olive oil. Fry bacon with garlic, chop finely and mix with cream. Stir into the spaghetti and heat gently. Just before serving, stir in raw egg and mix quickly through spaghetti.

CHICKEN À LA KING

❧❀❧

1½ cups cooked chicken, diced
1 16-ounce can cream of
  mushroom soup
1 packet frozen peas (or left-
  over cooked fresh peas)

Paprika
Sage
½ green pepper, minced
1 slice pimiento
¼ cup dry sherry

Add all ingredients, except sherry, to soup in a saucepan and simmer for 5 minutes. Add sherry and serve on fluffy rice.

CHICKEN AND HAM CASSEROLE

(Miss Pat Jarrett)

❧❀❧

3 dessertspoons butter
1 tablespoon shallots, chopped
3 slightly rounded tablespoons
  plain flour
¼ teaspoon pepper
1 teaspoon salt
¼ teaspoon paprika
1½ cups milk (or half milk and chicken stock)

½ cup cream
2½ cups cooked chicken
¼ pound ham, coarsely chopped
Buttered creadcrumbs
2 tablespoons grated cheese
Parsley
Mushrooms

Melt butter and sauté shallots until soft but not brown. Stir in flour, pepper, salt and paprika; cook 1 minute. Add milk and cream, stirring until sauce thickens. Cook 2 minutes longer. Fold in chicken and ham. Turn into greased casserole, top with breadcrumbs and grated cheese. (The casserole can be prepared beforehand up to this stage.) Bake in moderate oven (400°F.) until top is golden. Garnish with parsley, and sautéed mushrooms. Serves 5.

QUICK CHICKEN CASSEROLE
(Mrs Frank Dunworth)

❈

2 16-ounce cans cream of
  chicken soup
Cooked chicken pieces
1 pound lean ham, diced

1 16-ounce can asparagus,
  drained
½ pound mushrooms
¼ pound devilled almonds

Heat soup, but do not boil. Add chicken, ham and asparagus. Sauté mushrooms, add with almonds when chicken is hot enough to serve. Turn into casserole and keep hot in very slow oven (200°F.) until ready to serve. Serve on rice.

CHICKEN NAPOLITAINE
(Mrs James Craven)

❈

2 spin-chilled chickens
Salt and pepper
Olive oil and butter
2 onions, chopped
¼ pound mushrooms
¼ pound bacon, diced

2 garlic cloves, sliced
1 teaspoon rosemary
2 tablespoons tomato paste
2 tablespoons chicken stock
2 glasses white wine

Rub chickens with salt and pepper, put in saucepan of salted water, cover and simmer until tender. Heat oil and butter and fry onions until transparent. Add mushrooms, bacon, garlic and rosemary. Simmer until onion is soft. Stir in tomato paste and stock. Add wine, then chicken cut in serving pieces. Serve with fluffy rice and a green salad.

QUICK LUNCHEON DISH

❈

Slices of cooked ham
Slices of processed Swiss cheese
1 egg per serving

Salt and pepper
Cream

Place slices of ham in a shallow, greased ovenproof dish. Top each with a slice of cheese. Break in eggs without breaking yolks; season and top with cream. Bake in a slow oven (325°F.).

MOUSSAKA

1 or 2 brown onions
2 cloves garlic
4 to 6 tablespoons olive oil
2 pounds cooked lamb, finely
   minced
4 to 6 tomatoes
¾ pound mushrooms
2 tablespoons finely-chopped parsley

Salt and pepper
2 to 4 tablespoons tomato paste
6 tablespoons meat stock
4 to 6 eggplants
Flour
Olive oil
Parmesan cheese, grated

Sauté finely-chopped onion and garlic in oil. Add lamb and brown, stirring occasionally. Add chopped tomatoes, mushrooms, parsley, salt and pepper and cook until onion is tender. Dilute tomato paste with stock, add to pan and simmer for 10 minutes. Slice unpeeled eggplant into thin, lengthwise slices; salt, and drain on absorbent paper to remove moisture. Then dust with flour, sauté both sides in hot olive oil. Drain. Line a casserole with eggplant; spread layer of meat mixture and sprinkle with Parmesan cheese. Repeat layers, ending with eggplant and cheese. Bake in moderate oven (400°F.) until top is brown. This Greek shepherd's pie can be served hot or cold and reheats well.

ANYTHING MARENGO

(Mrs Max Cornelius)

2 large onions, chopped
Olive oil
2 large tomatoes

1 large sweet red pepper
Paprika
Salt and pepper

This is a sauce in which slices of precooked veal fillet or pieces of chicken can be heated. Lightly fry onions in oil. Cut up tomatoes; cut pepper into small strips and remove seeds. Add to pan and season with paprika, salt and pepper. Stir and simmer until ready to use.

FILLET OF BEEF

(Miss Dorothea Ganly)

❧✿☙

2½ pounds fillet of beef
1 dessertspoon olive oil
Cognac
Garlic (or bayleaf)
Parsley
Lemon juice

Soy sauce
Salt
Freshly-ground black pepper
Butter
Finely-chopped parsley

Marinate beef in oil, cognac (to taste), garlic, parsley, lemon juice, soy sauce, salt and pepper approximately twelve hours before cooking. When ready to cook, place fillet in foil with lots of garlic and butter, squeeze a lemon over it and sprinkle with parsley. Seal edges of foil and cook in moderate oven (400°F.) for about 1 hour.

PORK AND APPLE PIE

❧✿☙

About 4 pounds lean pork
4 to 5 apples, peeled, cored and
   thinly sliced
2 medium onions, finely chopped

1 teaspoon sage
Salt and pepper
Stock or bouillon
Mashed potatoes

Arrange alternate layers of chopped pork and apples in a deep baking dish. Sprinkle each layer with a little chopped onion, sage, salt and pepper. Moisten with a little stock or *bouillon*. Cover with thick mashed-potato crust and brush well with melted butter. Bake (325°F.) for 1½ to 2 hours. Serves 6 to 8.

ONIONS MONÉGASQUE

❧✿☙

2 carrots, chopped
4 tablespoons olive oil
2 pounds tiny onions
¾ pint water
¼ pint dry white wine
4 tablespoons lemon juice

2 tablespoons tomato purée
2 ounces sultanas
2 bay leaves
½ teaspoon thyme
Salt, black pepper and cayenne
Finely-chopped parsley

Sauté carrots in oil until soft and golden. Put in saucepan with rest of ingredients. Simmer 1 hour or until onions are cooked. Chill. Before serving, add olive oil to taste and sprinkle with chopped parsley.

PARTY SPROUTS

❖

Cook 1 packet of frozen Brussels sprouts according to directions. Drain and serve with 1 tablespoon melted butter, grated Parmesan cheese and chopped parsley. Alternatively, serve with 1 tablespoon of lemon juice and a grating of nutmeg; or sauté in butter with finely-grated onion.

MOCK WILD RICE

❖

Long-grain rice
Onion, finely chopped
Bacon, cooked and crumbled

Dash of nutmeg
Salt and pepper
Butter

Cook rice in salted water over very low heat for 25 minutes. Strain; season with onion, bacon, nutmeg and seasonings. Sauté in butter in a heavy pan until brown.

ANYTHING-GOES PURÉE

❖

Cook any frozen vegetables of your choice according to directions. Drain well and place in electric blender. Add 2 tablespoons melted butter, $\frac{1}{4}$ cup cream, salt and pepper to taste. Blend thoroughly at a low speed, then at a high speed until puréed.

Ideas from People in Vogue

MENUS

Lunch at a Holiday House
Mrs Walter Pisterman

Formal Dinner Party
Dame Mabel Brookes

Buffet Luncheon
CALIFORNIAN DESSERT CAKE
Mrs Malcolm P. Reid

Lunch for Overseas Guests
late Dr Eric Sussman

Summer Dinner Party
PEACHES IN CHAMPAGNE
Dame Zara Bate

Formal Dinner Party
CHEESE AIGRETTES
Mrs Simon Warrender

Lunch for Picnic Races
Mrs George Falkiner

Sunday Drinks and Lunch
Lady McIntyre

Dinner Party by a Career Girl
Miss Lou Sonnino

Luncheon at a Beach House
SEAFOOD CASSEROLE
Mrs Alan Copeland

✛✛✛✛✛✛✛✛✛✛✛✛✛✛✛✛

Starters
SALMON MOUSSE
Lady Potter

BLINIS WITH CAVIAR
Mrs Richard Austin

SPLIT PEA SOUP
Mrs Ken Mackay

Seafood Dishes
WHITING IN SAUCE DUGLÈRE
Mrs Wyndham Hill-Smith

ESCABECHE
Mr Carlos Zalapa

FILLETS OF JOHN DORY EN GELÉE
Baronne Yolande de Salis

PRAWNS IN SOUR CREAM
Mrs Peter Blaxland

Poultry
BALTIC GOOSE
Mrs Richard Austin

POULARDE MIMI TROTTIN
TURKEY PULLED AND GRILLED
Lady Harewood

CANARD SAUVAGE
Mrs Gordon Steege

ROAST CHICKEN WITH CHEESE
Mrs Ian Miller

CHICKEN FRICASSÉE
Mrs R. Seppelt

Meat Dishes
HAWAIIAN HOTPOT
Mrs Tom Hardy

GEFÜLLTE SCHNITZEL
Mrs George Récek

TABLELAND LAMB
Mr Grant McIntyre

VINTNERS' BEEF
Mrs J. Penfold Hyland

VEAL CLEMENTINE
Mrs Neville Palmer

ZRAZY ZAWIJANE
Mrs R. S. Zielinski

PORK FILLETS FANTASIE
Mrs Ian Baillieu

OXTAIL WITH BLACK OLIVES
Mrs David Wynn

Desserts
CHOCOLATE MOULD
Mr Cecil Beaton

PEARS IN RED WINE
Mrs R. Seppelt

SUMMER DESSERT
Mr Godfrey Winn

THE CONTENTS of this chapter first appeared in the pages of *Vogue Australia* and the editors are grateful to the experienced hosts and hostesses who have shared their own favourite party plans and treasured recipes so generously with our readers.

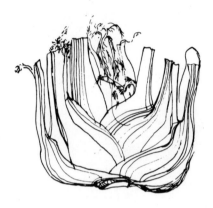

LUNCH AT A HOLIDAY HOUSE
(Mrs Walter Pisterman)

❧❀❧

MELON AND PROSCIUTTO HAM

MEAT CHEESE AND STUFFED HARD-BOILED EGGS

SLICES OF BABY VEAL SAUSAGE TOSSED IN FRENCH DRESSING
WITH FINELY-CHOPPED ONION

THICK SLICES OF BEEF FILLET

FRENCH BREAD WITH FAINTLY GARLICKY BUTTER

or

JELLIED TOMATO RING

ASPARAGUS, RADISHES, PICKLED CUCUMBERS, HAM AND
FRESH PINEAPPLE SERVED IN A DIVIDED DISH

This meal would be prefaced by Pimms mixed with equal quantities of soda and dry ginger ale, with mint, cucumber and lemon garnish. A chilled rosé would be drunk with the meal.

FORMAL DINNER PARTY
(Dame Mabel Brookes)

❧❀❧

PÂTÉ DE FOIS GRAS

LOBSTER NEWBURG
PUFFPASTE CRESCENTS

ROAST DUCK
ON PÂTÉ-SPREAD TOAST
GARNISH OF ORANGE, TOMATO, AND RED CURRANT JELLY ON FRIED BREAD

GRAVY MADE WITH RED WINE AND CHERRIES

GREEN PEAS   POTATOES

ICE CREAM ON CAKE
COVERED WITH MERINGUE AND BAKED GOLDEN BROWN, WITH
GARNISH OF CHERRIES, MARRONS GLACÉS, SCORCHED ALMONDS

FRESH PEARS

BUFFET LUNCHEON
(Mrs Malcolm P. Reid)

ICED TOMATO JUICE

SALMON MOULD
WITH CUCUMBER CREAM DRESSING

JAMBON FIGHI
(THIN SLICES OF HAM SURROUNDED BY PEELED FIGS)

CALIFORNIAN DESSERT CAKE

CALIFORNIAN DESSERT CAKE
(made the day before)

2 envelopes gelatine
½ cup water
8 eggs, separated
1 cup lemon juice
1 teaspoon salt
1 cup granulated sugar

2 teaspoons lemon rind, finely grated
1 cup granulated sugar
1 cup cream
2 3-ounce packets sponge fingers, split

Sprinkle gelatine over cold water to soften. Separate eggs; in top of double boiler combine egg yolks, lemon juice, salt, 1 cup granulated sugar. Cook over boiling water until custard coats back of spoon, then stir into it the softened gelatine and lemon rind. Allow to cool. Meanwhile, beat egg whites until they hold their shape; gradually beat in 1 cup sugar until stiff. Whip cream until stiff and pile on top of egg whites; top with cooled lemon mixture and gently fold all together. Line sides of 9-inch spring-form pan, with its round centre in place, with about 20 ladyfingers; spoon in lemon mixture. Refrigerate overnight. To serve, remove sides of pan and slide cake onto a platter.

LUNCH FOR OVERSEAS GUESTS
(the late Dr Eric Sussman)

Cocktail with Queensland rum

Australian dry sherry
KANGAROO TAIL SOUP

Hunter River white wine
STEAMED MURRAY RIVER COD
CUT INTO STEAKS AND SERVED WITH HOLLANDAISE SAUCE

FRESH GARDEN BEANS   TOSSED GREEN SALAD

Great Western champagne
TROPICAL FRUITS

SUMMER DINNER PARTY

(Dame Zara Bate)

❖

Dame Zara served this menu on occasions while she was châtelaine of 'The Lodge' in Canberra.

AVOCADO PEARS
WITH LEMON JUICE, OIL, SALT AND PEPPER

SADDLE OF LAMB WITH MINT JELLY

FRESH GREEN PEAS   SMALL BUTTERED POTATOES

FRESH PEACHES IN CHAMPAGNE

PEACHES IN CHAMPAGNE

Peel peaches, place in earthenware dish, cover with champagne and leave in refrigerator at least 12 hours. To serve, transfer peaches and their juices to a bowl and pour over them a fresh bottle of chilled champagne. The flavoured wine is ladled from the bowl into champagne glasses to drink while eating the peaches.

FORMAL DINNER PARTY

(Mrs Simon Warrender)

❖

CAVIAR

ROAST SADDLE OF LAMB

POIS FRANÇAIS   STUFFED TOMATOES

SAUTÉ POTATOES

GREEN SALAD

CHEESE AIGRETTES

LEMON SORBET *or* FRUIT IN MELON CASES

CHEESE AIGRETTES

2 ounces self-raising flour	1½ ounces grated Parmesan
1 ounce butter	cheese
¼ pint water	Salt
1 whole egg	Cayenne pepper
1 egg yolk	

Sieve flour. Bring butter and water to boil. Add flour; stir quickly until mixture comes away from sides of pan. Remove from heat; cool slightly. Add whole egg, then yolk, beating into mixture. Add cheese; season with salt and dash of cayenne. Turn on to platter to cool. (4 hours in coldest part of refrigerator improves taste.) Heat oil but do not let it boil. Drop teaspoons of mixture into oil, fry until golden brown. Serve on a napkin in a silver muffin dish.

LUNCH FOR PICNIC RACES
(Mrs George Falkiner)

❧❁☙

RICH BEEF CONSOMMÉ

CHILLED TOMATO SOUP, OR VICHYSSOISE*

COLD ROAST DUCK
WITH APPLESAUCE

COLE SLAW   HOT JACKET POTATOES

BUTTERED ROLLS

CHEESECAKE

*See 'Salads
and Outdoor
Meals' page 75

SUNDAY DRINKS AND LUNCH
(Lady McIntyre)

❧❁☙

CANNELLONI

GREEN PEAS   TOSSED GREEN SALAD

PEARS
POACHED IN CLARET AND TOPPED WITH WHIPPED CREAM

CHEESEBOARD
WITH CRACKERS AND CRISPBREADS

FRESH FRUIT

DINNER PARTY BY A CAREER GIRL
(Miss Lou Sonnino)

❧❁☙

VEAL IN MARSALA SAUCE

or

VEAL WITH ARTICHOKE HEARTS

TINY ZUCCHINIS, UNPEELED, PARBOILED, CUT IN
SLICES AND SPRINKLED WITH LEMON JUICE, CHOPPED PARSLEY

CANNED CHESTNUT PURÉE WITH CREAM

or

GRAPE JELLY

GRAPE JELLY

Heat a little ginger ale to boiling point, pour it over lime jelly crystals and
before it sets, fling in about 1 pound of whole, washed seedless white grapes.
Refrigerate.

34

LUNCHEON AT A BEACH HOUSE
(Mrs Alan Copeland)

❧❈❧

ICED PAWPAW *or* MELON

SEAFOOD CASSEROLE

HOT ROLLS   GREEN SALAD

CHEESE AND BISCUITS

SEAFOOD CASSEROLE

Combine cooked fish, lobster, prawns and oysters in casserole with the following tomato sauce. Stew peeled tomatoes in lots of butter with a squeeze of garlic, salt, pepper, a dash of sugar. Thicken with flour, then add milk and stir until smooth; add a dash of grated cheese. Pour over fish and reheat in oven.

❉ ❉ ❉ ❉ ❉ ❉

STARTERS

SALMON MOUSSE
(Lady Potter)

❧❈❧

2½ dessertspoons gelatine
1¾ cups hot water
1 teaspoon salt
2 tablespoons white vinegar
2 gherkins, finely diced

Chopped olives
1 tablespoon green pepper, diced
½ cup mayonnaise
½ cup whipped cream
16-ounce can salmon

Dissolve gelatine in hot water, add salt and chill. When slightly thickened, beat with eggbeater until of consistency of whipped cream. Fold in white vinegar, gherkins, olives and green pepper. Add mayonnaise, whipped cream and flaked salmon. Mix and turn into a mould (Lady Potter uses a fish-shaped mould); chill until firm; then turn on to bed of shredded lettuce and watercress. Serve garnished with green mayonnaise, with cucumber and tomato salad on individual plates.

BLINIS WITH CAVIAR

(Mrs Richard Austin)

❧❀❧

4 medium-sized raw potatoes	Salt
1 finely-chopped onion	Pepper
2 eggs	Caviar
Sweet cream	Sour cream

Peel potatoes, and grate finely; leave in bowl for some minutes until liquid rises to surface. Remove this with spoon and add onion, eggs, a dash of cream, salt and pepper to taste. Stir well and use as batter to make very thin pancakes about 4 inches in diameter, frying them in hot buttered pan until brown and crisp on both sides. Top each with caviar and a spoonful of sour cream.

SPLIT PEA SOUP

(Mrs Ken Mackay)

❧❀❧

3 pints stock	½ packet split peas
Ham, pork or mutton bone	Large handful fresh mint
3 rashers bacon	

Simmer all ingredients for about 4 hours until peas are puréed.

WHITING IN SAUCE DUGLÈRE

(*Mrs Wyndham Hill-Smith*)

⊰❖⊱

½ ounce butter
2 shallots, chopped
2 small tomatoes, peeled and
    sliced
1 slice lemon
Salt and pepper

4 whiting fillets
½ cup dry white wine
½ cup fish stock
Parsley
Beurre manié
Thin cream

Grease ovenproof dish with butter, put in shallots, tomatoes, lemon slice, salt and pepper. Lay fillets on top, pour on the wine and stock. Add parsley sprigs. Cook in hot oven 10 minutes. Lift fish on to hot serving dish; strain liquid into saucepan and heat. When boiling gradually stir in *beurre manié* (1 ounce butter and 1 tablespoon flour mixed together). Stirring all the time, cook very slowly for 10 minutes. Add a little cream or top of milk. Pour sauce over fish, garnish with chopped parsley.

ESCABÈCHE

(*Mr Carlos Zalapa*)

⊰❖⊱

(*This cold fish dish is an adaptation of a Mexican recipe*)

2 pounds schnapper fillets, boned
Batter and olive oil for frying
1 cup dry white wine
1 cup Spanish olive oil
1 cup vinegar
Mustard, pepper and salt

1 white onion
6 sweet gherkins
6 green olives
6 black olives
1 tablespoon capers
1 lemon

Cut fillets into squares of about 1½ inches. Make thin batter, coat fish and fry it in olive oil. Let cool. Make marinade of wine, olive oil and vinegar, seasoned with mustard, pepper and salt. Slice into it very fine rings of onion and gherkins. Add olives, capers and juice of ½ a lemon, slicing the other half finely into the sauce. Cover fish with marinade and let stand for about 2 hours before serving.

FILLETS OF JOHN DORY EN GELÉE
(Baronne Yolande de Salis)

❧❊☙

Aspic:

3 medium-sized schnapper heads	1 carrot, sliced
Fish trimmings	6 peppercorns
1½ pints water	Salt to taste
2 ounces wine vinegar	3 egg whites
1 bayleaf	

Simmer all except egg whites together for 15 minutes. Clear broth with egg whites, strain through muslin and set aside to cool. Then pour ¼-inch of aspic broth into a shallow, oval Pyrex dish, place in refrigerator to set. Reserve remainder of aspic.

Gently poach 6 John Dory fillets in a mixture of water, white wine, 1 small peeled onion, salt and *bouquet garni*. Let fish cool, then carefully remove skin.

Decorate jellied aspic in Pyrex dish with slices of stuffed olives and hard-boiled eggs; brush over gently with liquid aspic to secure decoration. Arrange fillets on the bed of aspic, cover with the rest of the liquid aspic broth and refrigerate until set.

Unmould on serving dish and serve with rémoulade sauce in a separate sauceboat. New Zealand fillets of sole, or filleted and skinned whiting can be substituted for John Dory.

PRAWNS IN SOUR CREAM
(Mrs Peter Blaxland)

❧❊☙

2 pounds small prawns, cooked	1 carton sour cream
½ pound white button mushrooms	Cayenne, garlic salt
Butter	Cornflour for thickening
½ glass sherry	Large *vol-au-vent* shells

Sauté peeled prawns and sliced mushrooms in butter. Pour on sherry; leave a while to marinate. Add sour cream, cayenne and garlic salt to taste. Before serving, heat and thicken with a little cornflour, mix to a paste with sherry. Fill into *vol-au-vent* shells preheated in oven for 10 minutes, and serve hot, with tossed salad. Serves 6.

BALTIC GOOSE
(Mrs Richard Austin)

❧✤☙

Clean an 8-to 10-pound goose and wipe with damp cloth. Tie neck with string and rub inside and out with pepper and salt. Stuff with 1 large apple, cored and cut into 6 pieces, and 12 each stoned prunes and apricots which have been soaked in brandy. Stitch up vent and prick bird well with a fork. Roast, breast-side up in oven (375°F.) about 2 hours until tender, basting frequently with pan juices to which a little hot water can be added if necessary. Pour off most of the fat and deglaze pan with port to make a light sauce. Serve with sautéed potato shells.

POULARDE MIMI TROTTIN
(Lady Harewood)

❧✤☙

1 chicken	1 glass dry vermouth
1 bunch fresh tarragon	$\frac{1}{4}$ pint thick cream

Stuff chicken with tarragon and roast it. Drain juices into saucepan and add to them the dry vermouth and cream. Stir over a low heat until sauce reduces and thickens; serve with chicken.

CANARD SAUVAGE
(Mrs Gordon Steege)

❧✤☙

Wild duck	Salt and black pepper
1 turnip	2 tablespoons dry white wine
2 carrots	2 cups stock
1 Swede turnip	Bouquet garni
4 shallots	1 orange, thinly sliced
Butter	$\frac{1}{2}$ pound green peas
Pinch of sugar	

Place larded wild duck in earthenware casserole. Cook until golden brown in a quick oven. Cube vegetables and sauté in butter with sprinkling of sugar, salt and pepper. Drain excess fat from duck. Add sautéed vegetables, wine, stock, *bouquet garni* and cook in moderate oven (400°F.) for 20 minutes. Add orange slices and peas. Return to oven until peas are cooked. Remove *bouquet garni* and serve with orange slices over the duck.

TURKEY PULLED AND GRILLED
(Lady Harewood)

❧❀❧

(This recipe for left-over turkey is a favourite post-Christmas dish at Harewood House, the Harewoods' country seat in Yorkshire)

Pull dark meat off the leg and marinate in a mixture of about ½ cup Worcestershire sauce, 1 cup olive oil, 2 teaspoons mustard, salt and pepper to taste. Chop the remaining white meat, mix with a béchamel sauce. Remove dark meat from marinade and grill it, then pile in the centre of a large dish, putting the white meat in sauce all around. Lady Harewood says: 'It makes a lovely contrast, the hot grilled meat and cold, bland white meat.'

ROAST CHICKEN WITH CHEESE
(Mrs Ian Miller)

❧❀❧

1 chicken
½ pound butter
Salt and pepper

1 ripe soft Camembert cheese
Breadcrumbs

Brush inside of chicken with plenty of melted butter, using a pastry brush; sprinkle with salt and pepper. Cut cheese into quarters and place these inside chicken. Brush skin all over with more melted butter, salt and pepper; cover with a thick layer of breadcrumbs. These eventually form a thick crust. Place in baking dish with melted butter or a little chicken fat beneath bird. Roast (400°F.) for 30 minutes. Take out and pour over top all melted butter remaining from brushing operation. Return to oven and baste every 10 minutes, tipping chicken forward to let some melted cheese run out of cavity for basting, until cooked. Serve with pan juices.

CHICKEN FRICASSÉE
(Mrs R. Seppelt)

❧❀❧

1 small roasting chicken
Salt and pepper
Butter
1 tablespoon flour
1 garlic clove, crushed
1 cup dry white wine
1 cup chicken stock
4 or 5 mushrooms

2 shallots, chopped
Bouquet garni
2 egg yolks
3 tablespoons cream
1 tablespoon unsalted butter
1 small lemon
Mushrooms

Cut chicken into serving pieces. Season with salt and pepper, sauté in butter in a skillet, turning pieces to brown on both sides. Sprinkle with flour. Add garlic, wine, stock and a little mushroom liquor obtained by boiling 4 or 5 mushrooms in a little water for 5 minutes. The chicken should be just covered by the liquid. Add shallots and *bouquet garni*. Cover, cook in moderate oven about 30 minutes, or until tender. Remove chicken to serving dish and keep hot. Reduce sauce to about half, take off the fire and thicken with 2 egg yolks beaten with 3 tablespoons cream and 1 tablespoon unsalted butter. Reheat gently. Add juice of 1 small lemon and a few cooked mushrooms. Strain sauce over chicken.

MEAT DISHES

HAWAIIAN HOTPOT
(Mrs Tom Hardy)

2 pounds lamb or hogget chops
Fresh pineapple, sliced
8-ounce can tomato purée
1 medium can mushrooms

Shallots
Herbs
Red or white wine

Pare as much fat as possible off chops and line bottom and sides of an oven-proof dish with them. Core some pineapple slices and lay on top of chops, seasoning layers as added until all chops and pineapple have been used. Pour tomato purée and mushrooms over dish, chop shallots and add, with some fresh or dried herbs. Finally, add wine so that level of liquid just reaches top layer in dish. Cook slowly (350°F.) until meat is tender. Serve with rice, or creamy mashed potatoes.

GEFÜLLTE SCHNITZEL
(Mrs George Récek)

4 large veal steaks
Salt and pepper
4 rashers rindless bacon
4 slices Gruyère cheese

Flour
Beaten egg
Breadcrumbs
Hard-boiled eggs for garnish

Pound steaks on each side; sprinkle with salt and pepper. Cover half of each steak with a rasher of bacon and a layer of cheese. Fold steak over and press edges together firmly, so that bacon and cheese are covered by meat. Roll in flour; dip in egg, then in breadcrumbs. Fry slowly for 6 minutes each side. Garnish each serving with sliced hard-boiled egg.

TABLELAND LAMB

(Mr Grant McIntyre)

❦✻❧

1 shoulder of lamb	Apple-garlic
Tomato sauce	Sage
Soy sauce	Rosemary
Dry white wine	Onion
Thyme	Sugar
Mint	

One or two nights, or even a week, before your dinner, cut the lamb into flat manageable pieces. Combine all other ingredients and marinate the meat in this mixture. The day on which you wish to serve it, scorch the lamb on a barbecue grill with flames and smoke from gum leaves and wattle twigs. Browned and blackened, the surface holds the unique bush fragrance for the next treatment. Put the lamb pieces into open casseroles with the marinade and extra stock, and leave in the oven (300°F.) for at least two hours. Serve with hot buttered noodles.

VINTNERS' BEEF

(Mrs J. Penfold Hyland)

❦✻❧

2 pounds stewing beef	2 tablespoons butter
Red wine	2 shallots, finely chopped
1 teaspoon thyme	1 garlic clove, finely chopped
1 bay leaf	2 tablespoons flour
2 sprigs parsley	⅓ pound bacon, diced
1 onion, sliced	6 to 8 small white onions
1 small carrot, sliced	

Cut beef into 1½-inch cubes, marinate for 24 hours in wine seasoned with the next 5 ingredients. Remove from marinade, dry with a cloth, brown on all sides in heavy pot with butter. Add shallots and garlic. Add flour and let it brown. Strain marinade and add to beef with enough stock to cover meat by more than half. In another pan lightly sauté bacon, then add to meat in pot. In bacon fat, brown small whole onions. Add these to pot, cover and simmer over low heat about 2½ hours.

VEAL CLEMENTINE

(Mrs Neville Palmer)

❧❀❧

4 veal cutlets	2 tablespoons butter
4 rashers bacon	1 large onion, sliced
Juice of $\frac{1}{2}$ lemon	1 garlic clove, crushed
Flour for coating	2 dessertspoons flour
$\frac{1}{2}$ cup grated cheese	$\frac{1}{2}$ cup white wine or stock
Salt and pepper	Thyme or capers

Flatten cutlets with meat mallet and remove rind from bacon. Rub each piece of meat with lemon juice and roll in flour and cheese. Add salt and pepper. Place each cutlet on rasher of bacon and roll up, bacon side out; secure with a toothpick. Heat butter and brown onion and garlic, then remove. Brown veal rolls on all sides and transfer to greased casserole. Blend flour into fat remaining in pan and brown lightly. Add wine or stock, stir until it boils. Return browned onion and garlic to pan, add a pinch of thyme or a few capers. Pour over veal rolls, cover and bake in moderate oven (400°F.) 55 minutes to 1 hour. Serves 4.

ZRAZY ZAWIJANE

(Mrs R. S. Zielinski)

❧❀❧

Round, or best topside steak, 1 slice per person	Onion, finely chopped
	Butter
Salt and pepper	4 tablespoons stock
Dry mustard	1 level dessertspoon flour
1 rasher bacon per person	1 to 2 dessertspoons sour cream

Cut slices of beef as for schnitzel and flatten with meat mallet. Sprinkle with salt, pepper and dry mustard. Place a rasher of bacon and some chopped onion on each slice of meat; roll up and secure with a toothpick. Sauté more chopped onion in butter until transparent; add rolls and brown on all sides, about 5 minutes in all. Remove and place in casserole. Sauté more onion until transparent, then pour contents of pan into casserole. Add stock, cover and cook in oven about 1 hour. When meat is cooked, remove rolls. Thicken sauce with flour; season and add sour cream if desired. Return rolls to sauce and heat through. Serve immediately.

PORK FILLETS FANTASIE
(*Mrs Ian Baillieu*)

⊹⊱❖⊰⊹

6, pork fillets
Chopped parsley
Crushed garlic, to taste
Salt and pepper
5 tablespoons butter

1 tablespoon flour
½ cup sour cream
½ jar cranberry sauce
2 tablespoons Cognac or brandy
2 apples, cored, cooked, and
    sliced

Trim fillets and pierce each end to make a hole through the middle. Stuff with parsley, garlic, salt and pepper. Fry quickly in very hot pan with 2 tablespoons butter; remove. Add rest of butter to pan; stir in flour and add milk, stirring until sauce is smooth. Return fillets to pan and simmer, covered, 25 minutes turning only once. When cooked, add sour cream, 2 tablespoons each cranberry sauce and brandy; test for seasoning and bring to boil. Arrange fillets on hot platter; place apple rings on each and cranberry sauce in the centre.

OXTAIL WITH BLACK OLIVES
(*Mrs David Wynn*)

⊹⊱❖⊰⊹

2 oxtails
2 to 3 tablespoons olive oil
Crushed garlic
4 to 6 tablespoons Australian
    brandy

1 large glass red wine
Stock
Bouquet garni
Piece of orange peel
Black olives, stoned and halved

Ask your butcher to cut oxtails into pieces. Heat oil in heavy casserole. Put in oxtail, fry it gently for a few minutes with crushed garlic to taste. Pour over warmed brandy and set alight (this is optional, but does strengthen the flavour). When the flames have died down, add wine, let it bubble a minute or two. Add just enough stock to cover pieces of oxtail. Bury *bouquet garni* and orange peel in centre. Cover, cook about 3 hours in very slow oven (250°F.). Pour off liquid into a bowl and leave until next day. Then skim off the fat, heat, pour back over oxtail. Add black olives. Cook 1 hour.

CHOCOLATE MOULD
(Mr Cecil Beaton)

❖

3 ounces butter
3 ounces cocoa
3 ounces ground almonds
3 ounces sugar
Hot water

1 egg
1 egg yolk
3 ounces petit beurre biscuits
Whipped cream
Mandarin orange slices

Heat butter and cocoa together, add almonds. Dissolve sugar in a little hot water, add to butter mixture. Beat egg and egg yolk and add. Cut (do not crumble) biscuits in small pieces; stir into mixture. Pour into mould and leave in cold place to set. Turn out, cover with whipped cream and slices of mandarin orange.

PEARS IN RED WINE
(Mrs R. Seppelt)

❖

6 fresh pears
1 pint red wine
2 whole cloves

1 small stick cinnamon, crushed
$\frac{1}{2}$ cup sugar
2 ounces Australian brandy

Peel pears and leave whole. Pour the wine over them; add cloves, crushed cinnamon and sugar. Cook over slow fire. Test with a wooden toothpick and when done, pour into a bowl and add brandy.

SUMMER DESSERT
(Mr Godfrey Winn)

❖

Sprinkle strawberries and slices of orange with brown sugar and white wine. Chill in refrigerator for 3 to 4 hours. Serve in scooped-out half melon shells.

Famous Fish Dishes

SOUPE DE POISSON (FISH SOUP)

SAUTÉED PRAWNS WITH HERBS

CREAMED CRABS

BRANDADE DE MORUE (PURÉED COD)

TUNA POACHED IN COURT-BOUILLON (FISH STOCK)

LOBSTER SOUFFLÉ

RAIE AU BEURRE NOIR (SKATE IN BLACK BUTTER)

THIS CHAPTER has been contributed by Madeleine Thurston, one of the best-known professional cooks in Sydney, where she ran a restaurant for some years and now operates a busy catering business. The recipes below, introduced with her own words, are adaptations of fish or seafood dishes that are famous in Europe and America. She has substituted fish available locally for those found only in northern hemisphere waters.

SOUPE DE POISSON

❧✿☙

'There are so many wonderful ways to prepare fish besides frying it: fish soup, for instance. I have marvellous memories of the fare on our South Coast farm when I was a child—with a father who liked to fish better than to farm, and a French mother who converted the catch into the following dish. (I have enjoyed identical soups in Greece and Italy.)'

1 cod's head (any large fish head)
2 pounds firm white fish, such as halibut
1 onion, chopped
1 leek, chopped
2 cloves garlic
4 sticks celery, chopped
Salt and pepper
1 tablespoon flour

½ pint milk
2 level tablespoons tomato purée (or 6 ripe tomatoes)
1 glass white wine
2 tablespoons finely-chopped parsley
1 tablespoon finely-chopped fennel
1 strip lemon peel, chopped

Place fish head and fish, onion, leek, garlic and celery in a large pan, season with salt and pepper, cover with cold water. Bring to boil and simmer until fish is soft. When cooked, lift fish out carefully, remove any bones, break into large pieces. Simmer the stock 20 minutes longer; strain; return to pan. Mix flour with milk to a smooth paste and add tomato purée and white wine; mix well. Add to fish stock and simmer, stirring until it thickens. Add chopped herbs and peel.

Place a piece of fish in each soup plate (the large, old-fashioned kind) and pour the soup over it. Serve with French bread and a watercress salad.

ROUILLE

2 cloves garlic
2 hot red peppers
1 slice white bread

2 tablespoons olive oil
¼ pint hot fish stock

In Provence, where they make this soup, they add *rouille* to it. To make *rouille*, pound garlic and red peppers in a mortar with white bread (from which the crusts have been removed) which you have dipped in water and squeezed dry. Blend to a smooth paste with olive oil, then thin to the consistency of heavy cream with hot fish stock. *Rouille* is a delicious side dish with any cold, poached fish or on slices of French bread. If fish stock is unavailable, it can be thinned with mayonnaise.

SAUTÉED PRAWNS WITH HERBS

❧❀❧

'When I lived in New York, I knew lots of pleasant fish eating places. *Gloucester House*, all delft blue and white, with scrubbed pine table-tops, served the most delicious entrée of prawns.'

Butter
4 large green prawns per person
Salt
Freshly-ground black pepper

Freshly-chopped parsley and
   fennel
Lemon juice

In a heavy pan, melt enough butter to cover the bottom of the pan generously. Heat gently and when butter bubbles, put in the prawns. (The prawns have a better flavour if cooked in the shell but are rather difficult to eat, so leave on the tail only.) Cook gently, about 5 minutes each side, until they are a good pink colour. Remove pan from heat, sprinkle prawns with salt and pepper, parsley, fennel and lemon juice.

The prawns can be prepared ahead, placed in individual ramekins and kept warm, but are best if eaten as soon as they are cooked. Hand around lots of bread to soak up the delicious lemon butter.

CREAMED CRABS

❧❀❧

'In Baltimore I discovered crab cakes, and a dish called creamed crabs which is a fine way of using the Alaskan crab meat now to be found in some of our fish shops.'

1 pound (or 2 cans) crab meat
1 tablespoon butter
1 tablespoon Worcestershire sauce
2 teaspoons onions, grated
1 small can champignons
1 teaspoon salt

3 hard-boiled eggs, chopped
$\frac{1}{2}$ cup celery, chopped
1 dash Tabasco
2 cups good white sauce
1 wine glass dry sherry
Grated cheese

Mix all ingredients with the white sauce. Flavour with wine and pour into a buttered casserole. Sprinkle with grated cheese and bake in moderate oven until golden brown.

BRANDADE DE MORUE

❧❀❧

'From America I went to France for three years, where a new (for me) fish dish was *brandade de morue*. This can be made here quite successfully with smoked fillet of cod, but salt cod fillets are readily available in Greek and Italian delicatessens.'

1 pound salt cod fillets
2 cloves garlic, crushed
6 tablespoons double cream
¼ pint olive oil

Juice and grated peel of ½ lemon
Freshly-ground black pepper
Toast triangles fried in olive oil
   or butter

Soak cod fillets in cold water for at least 12 hours, changing the water often. Place drained fillets in a saucepan, cover with cold water and bring to the boil. Remove from heat, cover saucepan and let cod simmer gently in water for 10 minutes. Strain cod, remove bones and skin, and flake fish with a fork.

Place flaked fish in electric blender with crushed garlic, 2 tablespoons cream and 4 tablespoons olive oil. Blend, adding the rest of cream and olive oil alternately from time to time until oil and cream are completely absorbed and the *brandade* has the consistency of mashed potatoes.

When ready to serve, simmer the mixture in a *bain-marie* or a saucepan over water. Stir in lemon juice and grated peel and add seasoning to taste.

Brandade de morue may be served hot or cold. If hot, place in a mound on a warm serving dish and surround with toast triangles fried in olive oil. If *brandade* is too salty, blend in 1 or 2 boiled potatoes.

POACHED TUNA (OR OTHER FISH)

❧❀❧

If you don't own a fish kettle, put fish on a rack over the *court-bouillon* and bring to the boil. Reduce heat and steam fish for 30 minutes. Leave to cool over the steam, firmly covered.

Break up the flesh and either serve cold with mayonnaise, or add to a hot, creamy parsley sauce.

A note of warning: even the most superb sauce cannot transform fish that is stale or overcooked. Always buy fish with firm skin and scales, and cook carefully to the point where the moist, opaque flesh can be easily flaked with a fork. Do not overcook, or it will lose its flavour.

LOBSTER SOUFFLÉ PLAZA-ATHENÉE

❧❀❧

'From the simple delights of poached fish I gradually worked my way up to the heights of that most exciting soufflé of lobster as it is served at the *Plaza-Athenée* in Paris. This recipe seems long and involved at first glance, but is well worth the effort. The quantities given will make 8 individual soufflés.'

Lobster Mixture

3 1-pound lobsters, or	1 tablespoon chopped chives
3 10- to 12-ounce tails	1 teaspoon paprika
¼ cup salad oil	1 cup heavy cream
½ cup carrot, finely chopped	½ cup Sauterne
½ cup onion, finely chopped	2 tablespoons Cognac
1 tablespoon finely-chopped parsley	

Lobster Sauce

3 tablespoons butter	½ cup heavy cream
3 tablespoons flour	½ cup dry sherry
1 cup milk	

Soufflé

5 tablespoons butter	6 egg yolks, beaten
6 tablespoons flour	½ cup Parmesan cheese, grated
2 teaspoons salt	6 egg whites at room temperature
Cayenne pepper	½ teaspoon cream of tartar
1½ cups milk	

1 To prepare lobster mixture, cut lobster and shell into large pieces (tail should be cut into three). Sauté lobster pieces, shell and all in hot oil in large pan, turning occasionally, for 5 minutes, until red. Remove to bowl.

2 Sauté the carrot, onion, parsley and chives in drippings in same skillet until onion and parsley are tender (2 minutes).

3 Return lobster to skillet. Add paprika, cream, Sauterne and Cognac and cook gently, covered, for 10 minutes.

4 Remove lobster, cut away shell and discard. Slice lobster meat ¼-inch thick; set aside.

5 Simmer cream mixture over medium heat, stirring to reduce to 1 cup. Force through a coarse strainer. Reserve for sauce.

6 To make lobster sauce, melt butter in small saucepan. Remove from heat, stir in flour until smooth. Gradually stir in milk.

7 Bring to boil, stirring. Remove from heat, stir in cream, sherry and reserved mixture.

8 Combine 1 cup sauce with lobster meat. Turn into 1½-quart soufflé dish. Reserve rest of sauce.

9 Preheat oven (375°F.).

10   To make soufflé, melt butter, remove from heat and stir in flour, 1 teaspoon salt, dash of cayenne, until smooth. Gradually add milk.

11   Bring to boil, stirring. Then, reduce heat and simmer until mixture becomes thick. Remove from heat.

12   With wire whisk, beat mixture into egg yolks; mix well. Beat in cheese.

13   In large bowl, beat egg whites with cream of tartar and salt until they are peaked.

14   With wire whisk fold egg whites, one half at a time, into egg yolk mixture until well combined. Pour over lobster in soufflé dish.

15   Bake in oven for 35 to 40 minutes, or until puffed and nicely browned. Just before serving, gently reheat the reserved lobster sauce.

RAIE AU BEURRE NOIR

❖

'Skate in the raw is discouraging. It is a hideous looking beast and that may have been against its popularity in Australia. It is, however, very good indeed, as well as economical.'

1 skate	Bayleaf
Water	Salt and pepper
2 to 3 tablespoons vinegar to each quart of water	Finely-chopped parsley
Several slices of onion	Butter
Bouquet garni	2 tablespoons vinegar
	1 teaspoon capers

Wash skate well and cut into suitable pieces. Place these in pan and cover with water. Add vinegar, onion, *bouquet garni*, salt and pepper. Bring to the boil slowly and simmer 80 minutes. Lift out fish and lay in a cloth; take off skin and keep fish hot in a dish. Sprinkle on parsley and salt and pepper. Melt butter in pan until it colours; pour over fish. Put vinegar in hot pan, add capers and pour this over fish. Serve with boiled new potatoes; follow with a French salad.

FISH COURT-BOUILLON

‐❧✿❧‐

'A recent discovery for me is tuna. I have never liked the tinned variety, but was interested in the size and texture of the fish at the fishmonger's and impressed by the amounts being purchased by other customers. So I ventured to buy it, and it is now installed high on my list of fine fish, delicious either hot or cold.

I poach it in a fish *court-bouillon*, which does for fish what a good chicken stock does for poached chicken.'

2 small carrots
2 stalks celery
1 large onion, sliced
3 tablespoons butter
3 tablespoons olive oil
1 pint water
1 pint dry white wine
1 teaspoon salt

2 pounds fish trimmings
  (any kind)
1 *bouquet garni* (celery, thyme,
  parsley)
2 bayleaves
6 bruised peppercorns
2 whole cloves

Sauté carrots, celery and onion, all finely chopped, in butter and oil until onion is transparent but not brown. Add water, wine and fish trimmings and bring to boil. Skim froth from liquid, add remainder of ingredients. Cover saucepan and simmer for 30 minutes. Strain and use as required. It will keep in the refrigerator, covered, for 2 to 3 days. Halve the recipe for small quantities.

5

Weekend Catering

Menus

A WEEKEND AT A HOLIDAY COTTAGE

A WEEKEND WITH HOUSE GUESTS

A WEEKEND ON A GOURMET DIET

A WEEKEND WITH TWO DINNER PARTIES

A WEEKEND ON THE BOAT

ALTHOUGH SOME RECIPES have been included in this chapter, we have concentrated on suggesting food *plans*. Some of these use recipes which appear elsewhere in this book, others include dishes which use the contents of your storecupboard. The menus have been based on the premise that weekends are for fun and leisure, so most of the suggestions are for food which you can prepare ahead and eat cold or reheat, or for quick dishes improvised from storecupboard supplies.

A WEEKEND AT A HOLIDAY COTTAGE

◆❧❀❧◆

We assume that your home-from-home has a refrigerator and a small stock of tinned foods, dry groceries and spices, therefore what is needed is careful preplanning of every meal. If you follow the strategy of spending Friday morning cooking food to take with you in the car, you can have a relatively chore-free weekend and still satisfy appetites sharpened by outdoor exercise.

Friday Evening

Since everyone will be tired after their long drive the suggested dinner menu requires little effort. The main course, cooked earlier that day, need only be reheated when you arrive.

AVOCADO PEARS
WITH VINAIGRETTE DRESSING

VEAL GOULASH
WITH NOODLES

or

FISH AND POTATO PIE

CHEESEBOARD

VEAL GOULASH

2½ pounds lean boneless veal
3 tablespoons butter
4 tablespoons Cognac
4 tablespoons butter
2 cups mixed carrot, celery and
    onion, sliced

2 tablespoons paprika
3 tablespoons flour
1 tablespoon tomato paste
2 cups chicken stock
Salt and pepper
1 cup sour cream

Cut veal into 2-inch cubes and brown a few pieces at a time, in 3 tablespoons butter. Flame with Cognac and remove meat. Add to pan 4 tablespoons butter and slowly sauté the mixed vegetables for 5 minutes. Mix in paprika, cook 2 minutes. Sprinkle with flour, mix, stir in tomato paste. Slowly stir in stock, mixing until smooth. Stir until it comes to a boil, season to taste. Strain sauce and discard vegetables. Return sauce to pan and slowly add sour cream. Replace veal. Cover and simmer 30 to 40 minutes or until veal is tender. Transfer to ovenproof casserole with lid and at the cottage reheat this gently (don't allow to boil). Serve with boiled, drained noodles tossed with butter and 1 teaspoon caraway seeds. Serves 4 to 6.

Dishes which you have prepared the day before can be served cold for lunch, leaving the only serious cooking of the day until evening.

Luncheon

RATATOUILLE

COLD KEDGEREE*

or

COLD TONGUE

FRESH FRUIT SALAD AND CREAM

*See 'Late Night Suppers' page 124

RATATOUILLE

1 medium eggplant	Salt and pepper
2 large onions, sliced	1 tablespoon finely-chopped
2 green or sweet red	parsley
peppers, diced	Pinch each of marjoram and
½ cup olive oil	basil
4 ripe tomatoes	1 small garlic clove
2 zucchini	

Peel eggplant, cut into ½-inch slices, salt slightly, pile together and let stand under a weight for 30 minutes to drain. Sauté onions and peppers in olive oil, in a large pan. As they begin to soften, add tomatoes (peeled, seeded and coarsely chopped), drained and diced eggplant slices and zucchini cut into ½-inch slices. Add salt and pepper, parsley, marjoram and basil. Simmer about 45 minutes or until vegetables are soft but not puréed, and liquid is quite reduced. Add a small, minced garlic clove towards the end of the cooking. May be served hot or cold.

Dinner

CHILLED SOUP
(USE A GOOD CANNED BRAND)

SADDLE OF LAMB

ROAST POTATOES   FROZEN PEAS

TOSSED GREEN SALAD

BANANES FLAMBÉES

Sunday

Brunch, rather than breakfast, to be eaten mid-morning, is an excellent idea for Sunday, when you and your guests must think of returning to the city. Luncheon can then be served late—perhaps at three o'clock—or alternatively, it can be made into a kind of 'high tea'; only a light supper need then be cooked when you reach home. The scalloped potatoes—like the veal goulash prepared on Friday—have only to be reheated.

Brunch

CEREAL WITH LASHINGS OF CREAM

SCRAMBLED EGGS

GRILLED HAM SLICES AND KIDNEYS

BUTTERED CRUMPETS AND HONEY

FRESH FRUIT

Luncheon

COLD LAMB WITH CHUTNEY

SCALLOPED POTATOES

CUCUMBER AND TOMATO SALAD

COFFEE FUDGE AND NUTS

A WEEKEND WITH HOUSE GUESTS

+⊲✦⊳+

Unless you organise yourself in advance, you may find yourself spending more time in the kitchen than in enjoying your friends' company. If they arrive on Friday, you may invite other people in to meet them and have drinks. The session can go on as long as you like if you have a favourite casserole simmering in the oven; we suggest one made the day before. Have a loaf of herb-sprinkled bread wrapped in foil to be crisped in the oven at the last minute, the fixings for a salad ready to be tossed in dressing, and some sherbet or ice cream in the freezer.

Friday Night

COQ AU VIN*

RICE HERBED BREAD

GREEN SALAD

LEMON WATER ICE WITH MANDARIN SLICES AND LYCHEE NUTS

*See 'Classic French Dishes to Cook the Day Before' page 88

Saturday and Sunday

On Saturday you may decide to go to the races, or spend most of the morning pottering around boutiques or art galleries. So plan an easily assembled, light cold luncheon. For Saturday night, vary the programme by taking your guests out to your favourite restaurant. Let yourself, as cook, off the hook on Sunday morning too: take a long leisurely drive, ending up somewhere pleasant for a late lunch.

Sunday night

QUICHE LORRAINE*

or

SEAFOOD CHOWDER

ARTICHOKE SALAD

CHEESE PLATTER

or

WARMED COFFEE CAKE

*See 'Salads and Outdoor Meals' page 75

This evening take out the pastry-lined dish already prepared for a *quiche* and fill it with the *Lorraine* mix (egg and bacon) or alternatively with ham and asparagus, or the Italian spinach filling. While it bakes, toss a lettuce salad in French dressing and add to it a can of drained artichoke hearts. A thick seafood chowder or *cannelloni* and cheese might be substituted for the *quiche*.

A WEEKEND ON A GOURMET DIET

❧❀❧

If your social life has been exceptionally active for a period and the results of so much hospitality—given and received—begin to show up on the bathroom scales, try a weekend of low-calorie meals. Let us hasten to say that the gourmet menus suggested in this chapter do *not* comprise a balanced weight-reducing programme: a weekend is far too short for that anyway. But even two or three days of this relatively Spartan régime could prepare you for going on a serious, planned reducing diet—and will leave you feeling and looking healthier come Monday.

For best results, begin on Friday, if possible. The breakfast menu below is the same each day. You skip lunch altogether; lay in some celery, raw cauliflower florets, radishes and so on to nibble, as between-meal snacks, if you must.

Breakfasts

FRESH RAW FRUIT

1 EGG BOILED, POACHED OR SCRAMBLED

1 SLICE WHOLEMEAL TOAST, LIGHTLY BUTTERED

BLACK COFFEE

Friday dinner

HALF GRAPEFRUIT

CRAB-STUFFED ZUCCHINI

CUCUMBER SALAD

YOGHURT

CRAB-STUFFED ZUCCHINI

4 zucchini (about 5 inches long)
2 shallots, minced *or*
  1 tablespoon onion, minced
1 tablespoon butter or oil
$\frac{1}{2}$ green pepper, chopped
1 medium tomato, chopped
$\frac{1}{2}$ teaspoon basil
$\frac{1}{2}$ teaspoon salt

$\frac{1}{4}$ teaspoon freshly-ground black
  pepper
1 tablespoon cornflour
$\frac{3}{4}$ cup dry white wine
1 teaspoon soy sauce
2 cups crabmeat (canned, frozen
  or fresh)
Few drops lemon juice
Grated rind of $\frac{1}{2}$ lemon

Scrape zucchini and halve lengthwise. Scoop out seeds, leaving $\frac{1}{2}$-inch shell. Put in saucepan, cover with boiling salted water. Cook 2 minutes, turn off heat and let stand 5 minutes. Drain. Sauté onion in butter until soft. Add green pepper, tomato, basil and seasonings and simmer 5 minutes. Stir in cornflower, then wine and soy sauce. Add crabmeat and heat through. Add lemon juice and rind. Fill zucchini with this mixture. Serve at once, or reheat under grill until sauce is lightly glazed. Serves 4.

Saturday dinner

SHISH KEBAB

1½ pounds lean leg lamb, cubed
1 cup buttermilk (or skim-milk
  yoghurt)
¼ teaspoon freshly-ground black
  pepper
Pinch of thyme

8 to 12 large mushroom caps
  (or 2 zucchini, sliced)
2 tablespoons oil blended with
  ¼ teaspoon salt
2 green peppers, cut in squares
8 to 12 cherry tomatoes
8 small onions

Place meat in large bowl and add buttermilk, pepper and thyme. Marinate for at least 1 hour, turning once. At the same time marinate mushroom caps or zucchini slices in seasoned oil, turning so all surfaces are well-coated with oil. Drain meat and arrange on skewers alternately with vegetables. Broil over charcoal, or under griller, until meat is browned and sizzling. Serves 4.

Sunday dinner

A WEEKEND WITH TWO DINNER PARTIES

⊶⧉⊷

If the seating capacity of your dining table is small, it is a good idea to have two consecutive dinner parties, on Saturday and Sunday. The beauty of this scheme is that you shop only once for food, flowers and wine, and cook for both parties at the same time. Make up two casseroles from the same recipe, the second to stay in the refrigerator for warming up on Sunday night. You can also duplicate the pudding, if you have one. Repeat the entire Saturday menu on Sunday, if you wish. But to avoid being bored by it yourself, the second time round, we suggest you change the first course and/or the dessert, and serve scalloped potatoes instead of rice with the casserole, or a different green vegetable.

Saturday's party

OYSTERS ON THE SHELL

MEAT OR CHICKEN CASSEROLE

RICE   GREEN VEGETABLE

TOSSED SALAD (OPTIONAL)

CHEESEBOARD AND BISCUITS

APRICOT MOUSSE*

*See 'Desserts with a Difference' page 110

Sunday's party

THE SAME AS SATURDAY'S
WITH A DIFFERENT FIRST COURSE
COLD SOUP *or* MELON AND PROSCIUTTO

INSTEAD OF THE MOUSSE:
FRESH FRUIT *or* CREME CARAMEL

A WEEKEND ON THE BOAT

Since the food storage, cooking equipment and washing up facilities are limited on most boats, and supplies of precooked food are quickly exhausted, any meals prepared on board must, of necessity, be simple and made from ingredients that do not spoil without refrigeration. Casseroles will only require reheating if they are taken on board straight from the oven and eaten soon after you are under way; fruit and salads can be washed and packed in plastic containers. Thin soups are best since they can be drunk from mugs, when the sea is choppy; if there is still a supply of ice by Saturday evening, cold *gazpacho* brought from home in a vacuum jug and chilled with an ice block in each plate is delicious with supper at sea in warm weather.

Saturday lunch

CHILI CON CARNE

GREEN SALAD

CRUSTY FRENCH BREAD OR ROLLS

FRESH FRUIT

CHILI CON CARNE

2 large onions, chopped
1 pound minced topside steak
1 dessertspoon chilli powder (or less or more, to taste)
1 bayleaf, crumbled
1 teaspoon oregano

1 16-ounce can whole tomatoes, peeled
1 to 2 16-ounce cans kidney beans, drained
Butter

Sauté chopped onion in butter until soft. Remove to casserole and in same pan, fry minced meat—adding more butter if needed—until browned. Sprinkle on chilli powder; the amount depends on how hot you like the dish to taste. Stir in well. Add bayleaf, oregano, and salt. Simmer a few minutes, then add the tomatoes and beans. Turn into casserole, mixing with onions, and cover; cook in moderate oven (400°F.) for 30 minutes to 1 hour. (This recipe is elastic: it can be eked out by adding 2 cans instead of 1 can of beans. Also, the cooking time can be lengthened if you wish.)

Saturday supper

HOT BOUILLON IN MUGS

FRANKFURTERS

CANNED SAUERKRAUT PICKLES

BOILED NEW POTATOES

CHEESE AND BISCUITS

Sunday brunch

PANCAKES WITH LEMON AND SUGAR

SAUSAGES, EGGS AND BACON

DATE LOAF OR OTHER LOAF WHICH CAN BE
EATEN WITHOUT BUTTER

COFFEE

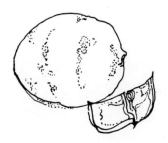

6

Salads and Outdoor Meals

Menus

BRUNCH IN THE GARDEN
QUICHE LORRAINE

SOUP AND SALAD LUNCHEON
VICHYSSOISE
SALADE NIÇOISE

LIGHT MEAL FOR A HOT DAY
JELLIED CONSOMMÉ
CHICKEN BREASTS SESAME

SOUTHERN-STYLE BARBECUE DINNER
GRILLED HAM STEAKS
CHARCOAL-ROASTED ONIONS

ALMOST-FORMAL OUTDOOR DINNER
TENDERLOIN STEAKS WITH
BÉARNAISE SAUCE

MIDSUMMER BRUNCH
CHICKEN LIVERS AND BACON EN BROCHETTE

SUMMER LUNCHEON FOR TWELVE
HAM BOURGUIGNONNE

LUNCHEON ON THE PATIO
APRICOT GLAZED HAM

Salads

SPRING GARDEN SALAD

BASQUE EGG SALAD

SPANISH TUNA SALAD

LOBSTER AND POTATO SALAD

CHICKEN AND LOBSTER SALAD

HAM SALAD

PRAWNS ORLÉANS

CHICKEN AND BACON SALAD

SPANISH SALAD

ONE OF THE DELIGHTS of summer in Australia is an alfresco meal on the terrace, by the pool, in a sheltered patio or beside the barbecue. Food for outdoor eating should be uncomplicated but appetising; no singed chops balanced on bread rolls. We have compiled some interesting menu suggestions, plus a selection of salads. Many of them would make one-dish meals for heat-wave weather, when one is inclined to limit cooking time.

BRUNCH IN THE GARDEN

❖

QUICHE LORRAINE

12-inch pastry shell	1 ounce butter
5 ounces bacon rashers	4 eggs
1 pint cream	Salt and pepper

Bake a pastry case in a 12-inch tin in a hot oven (450°F.) for 10 minutes. Cut rashers into ¾-inch strips and blanch in boiling water; dry them, and sauté lightly in butter. Set aside 6 of the best pieces and sprinkle the rest over the bottom of the pastry case. Whisk eggs and cream; add butter, then season to taste. Pour into pastry shell. Make a star on top with reserved bacon rashers and bake (375°F.) until custard is set and begins to brown on top. Serves 6.

SOUP AND SALAD LUNCHEON

❖

VICHYSSOISE

2 cups raw potato, finely diced	Salt, pepper, dash of nutmeg
4 tablespoons butter	1½ to 2 cups cream or sour
6 leeks	cream
3 cups chicken stock	Chopped chives

Cook potato in salted water to cover, until just tender. Cut white parts of leeks into 1-inch lengths. Melt butter in saucepan and sauté leeks for a few minutes. Add stock and bring to boil. Lower heat and simmer until leeks are tender. Strain and add potatoes and seasonings to liquid. Whirl in a blender, or put through a fine sieve. Chill. When ready to serve, mix in cream and garnish with chopped chives. Serves 6.

SALADE NIÇOISE

1 lettuce heart
½ pound green beans
½ pound new potatoes
Finely-chopped parsley

2 hard-boiled eggs
1 small tin tuna
2 ounces black olives
½ pound tomatoes

Cut lettuce in quarters. Cut beans in 1-inch pieces; cook in a little salted boiling water until just tender, and drain. Boil potatoes and slice thickly. Shell and quarter eggs. Flake the tuna. Stone olives. Peel and quarter tomatoes. Arrange ingredients in layers in bowl, beginning with beans and potatoes at bottom; tuna and tomatoes next; eggs and lettuce on top. Dot with olives, sprinkle with parsley. Pour over *vinaigrette* dressing just before serving.

LIGHT MEAL FOR A HOT DAY

❧❖☙

JELLIED CONSOMMÉ WITH CAVIAR

CHICKEN BREASTS SESAME

SAUTÉED GREEN BEANS

JELLIED CONSOMMÉ

Chill 2 16-ounce cans of beef consommé. Put a teaspoon of red caviar in the bottom of each soup cup, spoon on ½ cup of jellied consommé; top with a good dollop of sour cream. Sprinkle with chives.

Lovely

CHICKEN BREASTS SESAME

¼ cup melted butter
¼ cup soy sauce
¼ cup dry white wine
1 teaspoon tarragon

1 teaspoon dry mustard
6 boned chicken breasts
Sesame seeds

Mix butter, soy sauce, wine, tarragon and mustard. Marinate chicken in this for 2 to 3 hours. Grill over charcoal for 4 minutes each side. Remove from fire; brush with marinade, roll each breast in sesame seeds, return to fire to brown seeds. Serves 6.

SOUTHERN-STYLE BARBECUE DINNER

❧❀❧

GRILLED HAM STEAKS

CHARCOAL-ROASTED ONIONS

COLE SLAW

GRILLED HAM STEAKS

Slash fat around edges of 1-inch thick ham slices, brush with butter, grill over slow fire for 30 to 60 minutes.

CHARCOAL-ROASTED ONIONS

Allow 3 per person, wrap in foil with butter, salt, pepper. Cook in coals around edge of fire for 30 minutes. Serve with hot mustard.

ALMOST-FORMAL OUTDOOR DINNER

❧❀❧

TENDERLOIN STEAKS WITH BÉARNAISE SAUCE

NEW POTATOES WITH BUTTER AND CHIVES

GREEN BEANS WITH MUSHROOMS

BÉARNAISE SAUCE
(*for 4 steaks*)

2 tablespoons tarragon vinegar	3 egg yolks
2 chopped shallots	Cayenne
$\frac{1}{2}$ teaspoon finely-chopped tarragon	Salt
	$\frac{1}{4}$ pound butter

Heat vinegar, cook shallots until vinegar is absorbed, add chopped tarragon. Put egg yolks, dash of cayenne and salt in heavy bowl, add shallot mixture. Melt butter in a small pan. Place bowl containing egg yolks in double boiler over hot water, turn heat low. Whip egg mixture while adding butter gradually. When sauce thickens (almost at once), stir until thick and glossy. Keep hot over warm water until steaks are ready to serve.

MIDSUMMER BRUNCH

❧❀☙

CHICKEN LIVERS AND BACON EN BROCHETTE

MUSHROOMS IN FOIL

BAKED POTATOES WITH SOUR CREAM AND CHIVES

CHICKEN LIVERS AND BACON

3 chicken livers per serving
3 rashers bacon per serving
1 pound mushrooms

1 tablespoon butter per serving
Salt and pepper

Cut livers in half, wrap each in half a rasher of bacon. Thread on skewers; grill for 5 minutes over barbecue fire. Wrap mushrooms in 6 foil packages, with butter, salt and pepper. Lay around edge of fire for 10 minutes; turn, cook another 10 minutes. Open the packages with scissors and serve in foil. Serves 6.

SUMMER LUNCHEON FOR TWELVE

❧❀☙

COLD PLUM SOUP*

HAM BOURGUIGNONNE

TOMATO, ONION AND EGG SALAD

BAKED BEANS

MACÉDOINE OF VEGETABLES MAYONNAISE

COEUR À LA CRÈME†

*See 'Winning Starters' page 5

†See 'Desserts with a Difference' page 107

HAM BOURGUIGNONNE

1 10-pound cooked ham
1 veal knuckle
2 calf's feet, cleaned and split, or 1 packet gelatine for each 2 cups of liquid
2 bottles white Burgundy-type wine
6 shallots

Bouquet garni (2 carrots, 1 large onion stuck with 3 cloves, celery stalk with leaves, tarragon, chervil, garlic clove, 1 bay leaf, 10 peppercorns, all in a cheesecloth bag)
$\frac{1}{2}$ cup finely-chopped parsley
4 egg whites and crushed shells

The day before, place everything except the parsley and eggs in a large saucepan. Add enough water to cover ham. Cover and simmer slowly for $2\frac{1}{2}$ hours, or until ham is loose on the bone. Remove ham. Strain stock into clean saucepan. Clarify by adding slightly beaten egg whites and shells and simmering for 25 minutes. Strain carefully through a wet cloth. Bone ham and pack into serving bowl. When stock begins to set, mix with parsley. Pour over ham. Chill thoroughly. Before serving, remove any fat from top of jelly. Sprinkle with fresh parsley, slice and serve.

LUNCHEON ON THE PATIO

ARTICHOKES WITH VINAIGRETTE DRESSING

APRICOT GLAZED HAM

TOSSED GREEN SALAD

CHEESEBOARD   DIGESTIVE BISCUITS

APRICOT GLAZED HAM

1 4-pound cooked ham
$1\frac{1}{2}$ cups apricot nectar
1 cup applesauce
3 tablespoons Worcestershire sauce

$\frac{1}{4}$ cup chilli sauce
$\frac{1}{2}$ teaspoon dry mustard
Whole cloves

In large saucepan, sauté ham in butter over low heat for 10 minutes. Remove ham, score top and sides into diamond pattern. Return to pan and cook slowly 15 minutes, taking care to prevent it sticking. Combine nectar with all other ingredients except cloves; spoon over ham. Cover and simmer over low heat for 2 hours, basting well. Stud centres of diamonds with cloves. Serve on heated platter with sauce from pan.

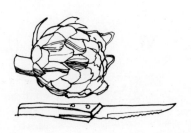

SALADS

SPRING GARDEN SALAD

+❖+

½ cup asparagus tips, cooked
   or canned
½ cup radishes, sliced
½ cup cucumber, sliced
1 cup lettuce, shredded
2 tablespoons green pepper,
   minced

4 tablespoons green onions,
   minced
1 tablespoon finely-chopped
   parsley
¼ cup Cheddar cheese, grated
¼ cup French dressing

Toss all ingredients together lightly. Serves 4.

BASQUE EGG SALAD

+❖+

2 cucumbers
6 hard-boiled eggs
4 pimientos, shredded
¾ cup black olives, halved
½ cup olive oil

Salt, freshly-ground black pepper
Pinch of dry mustard
1 teaspoon paprika (optional)
3 tablespoons cider vinegar

Peel cucumbers, cut in ⅛-inch slices, or into chunks. Put in a bowl, sprinkle with salt and let stand 20 minutes. Drain off liquid, arrange pieces in bottom of shallow serving dish. Place quartered eggs on top. Make border of shredded pimiento on top of eggs, scatter black olives in centre. Mix oil and seasonings; beat in vinegar until mixture emulsifies. Pour dressing over the salad about 20 minutes before serving. Serves 4.

SPANISH TUNA SALAD

+❖+

6-ounce can white-meat tuna
1 tablespoon olive oil
2 tablespoons dry sherry

1 small onion, cliced
2 tablespoons finely-chopped
   parsley

Drain tuna, add olive oil and remaining ingredients and toss lightly. Chill several hours before serving on lettuce. Serves 2.

LOBSTER AND POTATO SALAD

✥

⅓ cup olive oil
2 tablespoons wine vinegar
Salt, freshly-ground black pepper
3 cups boiled potatoes, sliced
½ cup cucumber, peeled and
diced
2 1¼-pound boiled lobsters,
chilled

⅔ cup mayonnaise
3 tablespoons heavy cream
¼ cup green onions, chopped
2 tablespoons finely-chopped
parsley
1 teaspoon lemon juice
Parsely sprigs or fresh basil
Tomato slices

In a mixing bowl, stir oil rapidly with a fork; add vinegar gradually. Add salt, pepper, potatoes and cucumbers. Stir gently and let stand 1 to 2 hours. Drain. Add lobster meat to potato mixture. Toss lightly. Add mayonnaise, cream, onions, parsley and lemon juice. Mix well; chill. When ready to serve, spoon mixture into chilled bowl. Add parsley or basil garnish, surround with tomato slices. Serves 6.

CHICKEN AND LOBSTER SALAD

✥

1 chicken breast, cooked
½ pound lobster meat
French dressing
3 hard-boiled eggs
1 cup celery, finely chopped
1 cup mayonnaise

2 tablespoons chilli sauce
1 tablespoon chopped chives
Salt, to taste
½ cup cream, whipped
2 cups cabbage or lettuce,
shredded

Cut chicken meat into small neat strips and dice lobster meat. Marinate in a little French dressing with chopped egg whites and celery for about 1 hour. Prepare and chill the following dressing: mash or sieve egg yolks and blend with mayonnaise, chilli sauce, chives and a little salt. Fold in whipped cream. Mix chicken and lobster with dressing and serve on bed of cabbage or lettuce in salad bowl. Serves 4 to 6.

HAM SALAD

✥

2½ cups cooked ham, cubed
½ cup celery, chopped
½ cup spring onion, chopped
¼ cup sweet pickle, or chutney,
chopped

Mayonnaise flavoured with
French mustard
Lettuce
Hard-boiled eggs
Finely-chopped parsley

Combine ham with celery, onion, pickle and bind with mayonnaise. Heap on bed of lettuce, surround with halved eggs and garnish with parsley. Serves 6.

PRAWNS ORLÉANS

❧❀☙

1 cup hock-type white wine
2 cups prawns
1 cup mayonnaise
1 tablespoon prepared mustard
1 teaspoon lemon juice
1 tablespoon finely-chopped
   parsley

1 tablespoon capers, drained
   and chopped
½ clove garlic, finely chopped
1 teaspoon grated onion
Salt and pepper
2 cups celery, finely cut
Lettuce leaves
Paprika

Pour wine over prawns (cut up, if large); cover and chill for several hours, stirring occasionally. Mix mayonnaise, mustard, lemon juice, parsley, capers, garlic and onion; season to taste. Drain prawns and dry by pressing between paper towels. Add them, with celery, to mayonnaise mixture. Pile into lettuce cups and dust each serving with paprika.

CHICKEN AND BACON SALAD

❧❀☙

3 cups cooked chicken, diced
½ cup bacon, fried until crisp
   and crumbled
1 cup cooked new potatoes,
   sliced

¼ cup celery, diced
1 tablespoon capers
Salt and pepper
French dressing
Salad greens

Combine chicken, bacon, potatoes, celery and capers. Season with salt and pepper, add dressing and serve on greens. Serves 4 to 6.

SPANISH SALAD

❧❀☙

3 medium-sized potatoes
French dressing
1 pound peas
1 small white onion

2 hard-boiled eggs
¼ pound cooked ham, in one
   piece
Mayonnaise

Cook potatoes in their jackets in boiling salted water until tender, about 25 minutes. Drain and when cool enough to handle, remove skins. Cut in small neat dice, marinate in a little French dressing and let stand until cool. Meanwhile, cook peas until tender, drain and cool. Peel and finely chop onion. Cut eggs into small cubes. Cube ham, cutting the pieces no larger than ¼-inch. Combine all ingredients and blend with mayonnaise.

7

Classic French Dishes to Cook the Day Before

THIS CONTRIBUTION to the cooking pages of *Vogue Australia* by Mr Tom Kernan, Editor-in-Chief of *Maison & Jardin*, and a well-known gourmet and host, deserves a chapter to itself. We have added suggestions for luncheon menus in which his own versions of five famous main-course dishes from the classic French cuisine could be incorporated. All of these taste better when made the day before they are to be served.

'On weekends at my house just north of Paris, my cook-butler Edmond both cooks and serves. So in the repertoire of his kitchen, it is important to have main dishes that can be prepared in advance, leaving him more time for the other entrées and for the table.

The following recipes have the added advantage that when chilled overnight, all fat can be removed before reheating, which leaves these substantial dishes lighter in texture and more digestible.

This concept of menus for Sunday lunch does not imply the least monotony. Here, as you will see, are five different dishes, made with lamb, beef, veal and chicken. All are French classics, but each can be uninteresting or, as Edmond makes them, can be very, very good.

All quantities given are for six persons. In all recipes, *bouquet garni* means a sprig of thyme, a bay leaf, the leafy end of a branch of celery and several sprigs of fresh parsley, tied together with a thread and removed before reheating. Pepper is always freshly ground from a mill. Parsley also should be fresh. Whenever you use garlic, take a fork and crush the amount needed into a cream with a bit of salt before adding it to the pot. In this way an unsuspecting guest can't bite into a clove of it. And do not say "my husband doesn't like garlic", for in this way he will never know it is there.'

I

SMOKED SALMON
or
SLICES OF PEPPERY SALAMI AND SMOKED PORK WITH GHERKINS

LA BLANQUETTE DE VEAU

PETIT POIS

WATERCRESS SALAD

FRESH TROPICAL FRUIT

COFFEE

LA BLANQUETTE DE VEAU

2 pounds breast of veal
2 pounds shoulder of veal
1 quart water
Bouquet garni
2 large carrots, diced
2 small turnips, sliced
2 medium onions, each studded
   with several cloves
Lemon juice
1 pound mushrooms, sliced

3 tablespoons flour
3 tablespoons butter
1 cup sour cream
$\frac{1}{4}$ teaspoon nutmeg
Salt, white pepper
2 egg yolks
1 tablespoon finely-chopped
   parsley
1 tablespoon finely-chopped
   chervil

Cut veal into 2-inch pieces and put in large enamel pan with water. Bring to a hard boil at least twice and carefully skim off all the scum that rises to the surface. Remove the pieces of meat and rinse in cold water; return to the broth, add enough water to cover well, put in the *bouquet garni*, carrots, turnips and onions. Cover and bring to a slow boil for $1\frac{1}{4}$ hours, or until veal seems well-cooked. Remove the pieces of meat with a perforated spoon, sprinkle with lemon juice to keep from darkening, cover with foil. Strain the consommé through a sieve, discard the vegetables and return to stove; drop in mushrooms, simmer for ten minutes. Remove from liquid, sprinkle with lemon juice. Put the three dishes—meat, mushrooms, consommé—into the refrigerator overnight.

Next day, thoroughly degrease liquid. In another casserole, make a roux with flour and butter and consommé. If there is insufficient liquid add canned chicken stock. Slowly blend in liquid so that it is quite smooth. When it begins to thicken, pour in sour cream and add nutmeg. Test for seasoning. Put in pieces of veal and mushrooms, simmer until heated through. Shortly before serving, stir in beaten egg yolks to thicken the sauce. Fold in parsley and chervil. Keep hot until ready to serve. Do not boil.

2

BEETROOT SALAD WITH CAPERS

LE COQ AU VIN

SCALLOPED POTATOES

CHEESEBOARD

DIGESTIVE AND WATER BISCUITS

SLICED PRESERVED ORANGES

or

ORANGES ORIENTALE*

*See 'Desserts with a Difference' page 107

LE COQ AU VIN

1 5-pound rooster
4 tablespoons butter
2 tablespoons oil
$\frac{1}{4}$ cup brandy
6 ounces smoked bacon, diced
6 ounces salt pork, diced
12 small onions

Bouquet garni, with extra thyme
1$\frac{1}{2}$ bottles red wine
1 16-ounce can chicken or beef consommé
4 tablespoons tomato paste
1 clove garlic
Cornflour

Cut rooster (or 2 smaller birds, if you prefer) into serving pieces. Sear pieces in a heavy casserole in the sizzling butter and oil. When all the pieces are golden brown, pour in brandy, ignite it and spoon the flaming liquid over meat until the flame dies down.

Take out chicken and keep warm; in the same fat sauté the bacon and pork until well-browned. Remove and add to chicken. Lastly, in the same skillet, brown the onions.

Return everything to the casserole with the *bouquet garni* and pour in red wine. Cook over a low heat for about two hours, or in the oven if you have a lidded casserole. When chicken is sufficiently done, put casserole in a cool place, then refrigerate overnight. The day before, you can also prepare the sauce for blending into the final cooking: simmer together canned consommé, tomato paste and creamed garlic for 15 minutes.

Next day, degrease the casserole. Add tomato sauce. Cook together on a low fire for about 10 minutes after reaching a low boil. If sauce is not thick enough, stir in 1 or more tablespoons of cornflour previously diluted in some of the liquid. Test for seasoning; serve in a deep dish.

3

PRAWN COCKTAIL
NAVARIN DE MOUTON
MIXED SALAD
TREACLE TART AND CREAM
TURKISH COFFEE

NAVARIN DE MOUTON

❦❖❧

1½ pounds breast of lamb
1½ pounds shoulder of lamb
4 tablespoons butter
1 tablespoon oil
1½ tablespoons flour
2 cloves garlic
2 teaspoons salt
2 cups beef stock

1 tablespoon tomato paste and
    one cup of stock
or ¾ pound ripe tomatoes
Bouquet garni
12 small onions
Freshly-ground black pepper
½ pound dry white navy beans
1 large onion, chopped
1 tablespoon tomato paste

Cut lamb into 1½-inch cubes. Brown the pieces over a hot fire in butter and oil. Drain off and reserve butter. Sprinkle meat with flour, return to heat and stir in garlic which has been crushed into the salt. Add beef stock and tomato paste diluted in another cup of stock, or, during the summer season, ripe tomatoes, skinned seeded and cut into small pieces. Add a *bouquet garni.*

While this is coming to the boil, heat in a separate skillet the previously reserved fat. Put in the onions and when they are golden add, with rest of fat, to casserole. Grind in pepper to taste. Let the stew simmer on the stove or in a preheated oven. When the meat is done (about an hour later) cool and refrigerate overnight.

Meanwhile, soak the white navy beans in water. Cook until nearly soft (about 1½ hours) with the large onion. Drain and refrigerate overnight.

Next day, degrease stew and remove the *bouquet garni*. Add another tablespoon of tomato paste. Bring stew to the boil and pour in the nearly-cooked beans. Heat for 5 to 10 minutes, or until beans are well done, but not mushy.

4

BOEUF À LA BOURGUIGNONNE

MARINADE:

1 medium onion, chopped
1 rib celery, chopped
1 large carrot, scraped
1 small clove garlic, mashed with salt

1 cup dry white wine
$\frac{1}{2}$ cup water
Bouquet garni

$2\frac{1}{2}$ pounds round steak
3 tablespoons butter
1 cup red wine
1 pound carrots, chopped
1 large onion, chopped

$\frac{1}{2}$ pound mushrooms, sliced
$1\frac{1}{2}$ tablespoons flour
2 tablespoons finely-chopped
    parsley

Make the marinade as follows: mix all marinade ingredients together and simmer, covered, for 15 minutes.

While the marinade is cooling slightly, cut the steak into $1\frac{1}{2}$-inch cubes, removing all fat. Soak in the marinade 2 or 3 hours, turning the pieces several times. Remove from marinade and drain on strainer until almost dry. Brown 2 or 3 pieces of meat at a time in butter in a heavy casserole. Put aside in a warm oven. Strain the marinade, pour into the butter remaining in the casserole; add the red wine; return the pieces of meat when the liquid comes to boil; add carrots and onion. Cover and bake in oven (350°F.) until meat is tender, approximately $2\frac{1}{2}$ hours. Refrigerate overnight.

The next day, remove the surface grease, bring to the simmer and add the mushrooms. Cook 15 minutes. Blend flour into a little of the sauce, stir into the hot mixture and cook, stirring constantly, until slightly thickened. Sprinkle with parsley and serve.

5

*See 'Winning
Starters'
page 5

MOCK MULLIGATAWNY*

or

TOHEROA SOUP

BOEUF À LA MODE EN GELÉE

CORN ON THE COB

SALAD OF FENNEL

or ENDIVE, WITH FRENCH DRESSING

ICE CREAM WITH PRESERVED GINGER

COFFEE

BOEUF À LA MODE EN GELÉE

◦⧃╬⧁◦

MARINADE:
2 carrots, sliced
2 onions, chopped
2 celery ribs, chopped
1 clove garlic
Bouquet garni

3 cups strong red wine
$\frac{1}{2}$ cup olive oil
Juice of $\frac{1}{2}$ lemon
Finely-chopped parsley

3 pounds boneless beef
Salt and pepper
4 tablespoons oil
$\frac{1}{4}$ cup brandy
$2\frac{1}{2}$ cups beef stock *or*
  1 16-ounce can beef consommé

Boned calf's foot
3 ounces bacon rind
1 pound carrots, evenly sliced
12 small white onions

If possible, have the beef larded, or do it yourself. However, it is not essential. Rub it with salt and pepper; trim and tie for cooking; marinate overnight in the marinade mixture, smearing it over all sides of meat which should be turned at least twice. In the morning, drain on a rack and dry with paper towels. Heat the oil in a heavy ovenproof casserole and brown meat all over, turning as required. Pour in brandy, ignite and spoon over meat until flame goes out. Remove cooking fat and pour in unstrained marinade. Add beef stock or canned consommé, the calf's foot, bacon rind cut into tiny pieces (which have been boiled in unsalted water for 10 minutes). When all this has come to the boil, put into a preheated oven (350°F.) and let simmer about 3 hours, or until a fork pierces it easily. Meanwhile, boil carrots and onions until tender (preferably in beef stock); drain and set aside.

When meat is done, remove and drain it; immediately strain the cooking liquid and set in coldest part of refrigerator so fats will rise to the surface. When this is done, degrease; boil down liquid to make about 2 cups. The calf's foot will give some gelatinous quality, but it is better to add an envelope of unflavoured gelatine.

In the meantime the beef will have chilled. Untie, trim and slice about $\frac{1}{3}$-inch thick. In a large flat dish make a bottom layer of carrots and onions cut in two, arranged geometrically; pour a thin layer of the gelatine liquid over them; let it set. Assemble the slices of meat and place them carefully on the carrots; you may, if you wish, put several carrot slices between each slice of meat. Add the rest of the onions. Pour in more gelatine, let it set, add more carrots and more liquid until the mould is completely filled. Immediately before serving unmould on to a platter and sprinkle with parsley. Chop any left-over jelly and pile around the meat.

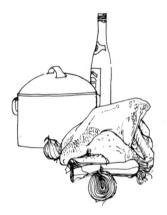

Home-made Breads

BASIC WHITE BREAD

KNEADLESS BREAD

IRISH BROWN BREAD

BEER BREAD

BAKING POWDER STOLLEN

CARAWAY RYE BREAD

CREAM CHEESE ROLLS

HARVEST LOAF

CARAWAY MELBAS

IRISH BARMBRACK

PAIN D'ÉPICE

EASTER GINGERBREAD

In most Australian households, bread-making has become almost a lost art. This is a pity, because nothing is more delicious than fragrant, crusty home-baked loaves fresh from the oven. Yeast breads are made from either compressed yeast, which will keep for about a week in a refrigerator, or the granular type which stays fresh for months. Yeast should be dissolved in warm liquid, and left to rise in a warm, draught-free place. After mixing the dough, put a damp cloth over the bowl to prevent the surface drying out. Do not let it rise too long: to test, poke a finger in the dough. If the mark remains, it has risen sufficiently. Bake in a hot oven to 'kill' the yeast.

Yeast breads may take time, but soda breads are made in minutes, and require a light touch. Mix the dry and liquid ingredients until they are just moistened, and do not be dismayed if the batter looks lumpy; overmixing produces unevenly textured bread. Since it is leavened with bicarbonate of soda or baking powder, it should be mixed, rolled out and put quickly in the oven before the leavening gas can escape.

BASIC WHITE BREAD

⬥❖⬥

2 ounces yeast
1¼ cups warm water
1 cup lukewarm milk
3 tablespoons sugar
1 tablespoon soft butter

2 tablespoons vegetable oil
  (not olive)
2 tablespoons salt
7 cups plain flour

Dissolve yeast in ⅓ cup of warm water and combine remaining water with milk, sugar, butter, oil and salt. Add yeast and flour to make soft dough. Knead on floured pastry board. Place dough in greased bowl and cover. Let rise in warm place for 1 hour or until dough doubles in bulk. Punch down and knead lightly. Let rise for another 30 minutes. Cut dough in half and leave for 10 minutes. Shape each half into a loaf. Place in greased tins, cover and allow to rise for 30 minutes. Bake 25 minutes in preheated oven (425°F.) or until loaves sound hollow when tapped. Take out of tins and cool on a rack.

KNEADLESS BREAD

⬥❖⬥

1 ounce yeast
1¼ cups warm water
2 tablespoons melted butter
2 tablespoons salt

2 tablespoons sugar
⅓ cup wheat germ
2⅔ cups plain flour

Dissolve yeast in warm water in a bowl. Add butter, salt, sugar, wheat germ and 1 cup of flour. Beat thoroughly. Add 1⅔ cups flour gradually. Beat with wooden spoon until dough leaves the sides of the bowl and spoon is clean. Cover bowl and set in a warm place to rise for 1 hour. Spoon dough into 2 well-greased tins and set in warm place to rise for 40 minutes. Bake in pre-heated oven (375°F.) for 45 minutes.

IRISH BROWN BREAD

⬥❖⬥

½ teaspoon salt
½ teaspoon bicarbonate of soda
½ pound plain flour

1 ounce butter
2 tablespoons oatmeal
Sour cream or buttermilk

Sieve together salt, soda and flour. Rub in butter. Mix in the oatmeal; add sufficient thin sour cream to make a soft dough. Knead into a round cake on a floured board and bake 30 minutes in a preheated oven (375°F.)

BEER BREAD

·⊰❋⊱·

1 cup beer	2 cups plain flour
1 ounce yeast	1 cup wholemeal flour
½ cup brown sugar	½ cup wheat germ
2 tablespoons melted butter	½ teaspoon salt

Heat beer to lukewarm. Remove from heat and sprinkle with the yeast. Add brown sugar and leave in warm place for 5 minutes. Add yeast mixture to butter, flours, wheat germ and salt. Knead and follow rising method as for basic white bread. Bake (375°F.) for 1 hour.

BAKING POWDER STOLLEN

·⊰❋⊱·

1⅔ cups plain flour	½ cup candied orange peel,
1½ teaspoons baking powder	chopped
6 tablespoons sugar	½ cup candied cherries, chopped
½ teaspoon mace	⅓ cup ground almonds
½ teaspoon nutmeg	1 egg
¼ teaspoon salt	½ teaspoon vanilla essence
⅓ cup butter	1 tablespoon melted butter
⅔ cup cottage cheese	¼ cup icing sugar
½ cup raisins	

Mix together first 12 ingredients. Make a well in centre and drop in egg and vanilla. Knead to smooth dough. Pat out to a rectangle 6 inches by 10 inches. Fold over ⅓ of dough from the long side to make a loaf 4 inches by 10 inches. Place on greased baking tin and bake in preheated oven (325°F.) for 45 minutes. Brush top with melted butter and dust with icing sugar. Cool on a rack, wrap in foil and refrigerate 2 weeks before using.

CARAWAY RYE BREAD

·⊰❋⊱·

2 ounces yeast	2½ pounds plain flour
3 ounces golden syrup	2½ pounds rye flour
1 teaspoon sugar	½ ounce caraway seeds
3 pints warm water	2 teaspoons salt

Dissolve yeast, syrup and sugar in warm water. Add remaining ingredients to make a soft, smooth dough. Let rise for 1 hour in warm place. Knead and let rise for a further hour. Knead the shape into loaves and bake in a pre-heated oven (375°F.) for 35 minutes. This bread is best eaten the next day.

CREAM CHEESE ROLLS

❧❀☙

1 teaspoon sugar
¼ cup lukewarm water
1 ounce yeast
2 tablespoons sugar
¼ cup butter
4 eggs, beaten
1 teaspoon salt
¾ cup warm milk

4 cups plain flour
2 cups cream cheese
2 egg yolks
1 whole egg
1 tablespoon melted butter
2 tablespoons sour cream
2 tablespoons sugar
½ cup raisins

Dissolve 1 teaspoon sugar in lukewarm water. Add yeast and leave 15 minutes. Cream sugar and ¼ cup butter. Add beaten eggs, salt and warm milk. Stir in yeast mixture. Add 2 cups flour and beat until smooth. Add 2 more cups flour. Knead on floured board until smooth. Place in greased bowl and let rise for 1 hour. Punch down and form into small buns. Place on greased baking sheet and let rise 45 minutes. Make a depression in middle of each bun and fill with mixture of last 7 ingredients. Let rise for 10 minutes and bake 25 minutes in preheated oven (350°F.).

HARVEST LOAF

❧❀☙

1 teaspoon salt
2 cups warm water
1 packet dry yeast
7 cups sifted flour

2 tablespoons melted
  shortening
1 egg beaten with 1 tablespoon
  water

Put salt in 3-quart bowl and dissolve in water which is comfortably hot to the hand. Sprinkle yeast over surface. When dissolved, add 2 cups of flour and let rise in warm place until bubbly (about 1 hour). Add balance of flour and shortening, and knead until very small and elastic. This will be a very stiff dough. Put into bowl, cover closely with plastic wrap and let rise in a warm place until doubled in bulk (about 1½ hours). Remove covering and punch down. Cover again and let rise for about 1 hour. At end of this period, the dough will be ready to shape. To make a harvest loaf or plaque, roll out rested dough ¼ inch thick. Transfer to greased cookie sheet. Lay an inverted, floured plate on it and cut around the plate with sharp knife. Remove excess dough and the plate. Set aside to rise at room temperature while you prepare decorations from excess dough. Form sunburst or little figures and as each is formed put on a plate and cover with plastic wrap to prevent drying. When all are ready, assemble the composition, moistening either the loaf or the pieces with water to make them stick. Immediately place loaf in a preheated oven (425°F.). After 10 minutes the surface should be dry and set. Take loaf from oven and carefully brush surface with the egg wash. Return to oven and bake about 20 minutes until sufficiently brown.

CARAWAY MELBAS

⊹⊹❈⊹⊹

4 very thin slices of seedless rye
   bread

2 teaspoons soft butter
$1\frac{1}{2}$ teaspoons caraway seeds

Place bread on baking sheet, spread carefully with butter and sprinkle with caraway seeds. Bake in preheated oven (325°F.) for about 25 minutes, or until dry and crisp. (Baking time will vary, depending on dryness of bread and thickness of slices.)

IRISH BARMBRACK

⊹⊹❈⊹⊹

1 pound dried fruit
$\frac{1}{2}$ cup brown sugar
1 cup cold tea (milkless)

2 cups self-raising flour
1 egg, lightly beaten

Overnight, soak together dried fruit (currants, sultanas, candied peel, whatever you have) and brown sugar in tea. In morning add flour and lightly beaten egg. Mix well together; bake in a bread tin for $1\frac{1}{2}$ to 2 hours in preheated oven (350°F.). When cold, cut into thin slices like a fruit loaf. Serve well buttered.

PAIN D'ÉPICE

⊹⊹❈⊹⊹

Prunes, candied cherries, canned
   pineapple
3 tablespoons butter
$\frac{3}{4}$ cup dark brown sugar
1 whole egg
1 egg yolk
$\frac{3}{4}$ cup brown corn syrup

$\frac{3}{4}$ cup strong black coffee
$1\frac{1}{2}$ teaspoons cinnamon
$1\frac{1}{2}$ teaspoons soda
$\frac{3}{4}$ teaspoon salt
5 cups sifted flour
2 cups mixed raisins, currants
   and almonds, chopped

Soak prunes overnight. In morning remove pits, taking care not to spoil shape of prunes. Arrange prunes, cherries and pineapple in well-buttered, fluted 3-quart mould, filling in the hollows in the bottom of the pan with the fruit. Blend butter and brown sugar in large bowl of electric mixer. Add egg and egg yolk and beat until light. Mix corn syrup and coffee in another bowl. Mix and sift cinnamon, soda and salt with $4\frac{3}{4}$ cups of the flour. Mix chopped fruits and nuts with remaining $\frac{1}{4}$ cup of flour. Add sifted, dry ingredients to egg mixture, alternating with the liquids. When thoroughly blended, fold in the raisin and nut mixture. Spoon batter carefully into prepared mould. Bake in preheated oven (325°F.) for $1\frac{1}{4}$ to $1\frac{1}{2}$ hours, or until bread shrinks from sides of pan.

EASTER GINGERBREAD

❖

2 tablespoons golden syrup
1½ ounces brown sugar
2 ounces butter
6 ounces plain flour
½ teaspoon cinnamon
1 teaspoon ground ginger
¼ teaspoon ground cloves

Pinch of salt
1 ounce crystallised ginger
1 ounce candied peel, chopped
1 egg, beaten
¼ teaspoon bicarbonate of soda
2 tablespoons warm milk

Melt syrup, sugar and butter slowly in a saucepan. Add flour, spices, salt, ginger and candied peel, and beat well. Add egg and mix thoroughly, before adding bicarbonate of soda dissolved in warm milk. Bake in slow oven (350°F.) about 1 hour.

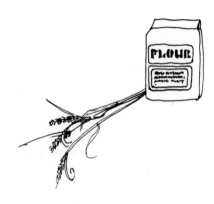

9

Desserts with a Difference

Served cold:

ORANGES ORIENTALES

COEUR À LA CRÈME

RUM SOUR-CREAM MOUSSE

FIGS CHANTILLY

APRICOT COINTREAU

COFFEE LIQUEUR FOAM

ORANGE SHERBET

RUM SOUFFLÉ

MOCHA MARSHMALLOW

CRÈME PARISIENNE

APRICOT MOUSSE

SACHER TORTE

BISCUIT TORTONI

COFFEE SPONGE

PEACHES STUFFED WITH MACAROONS

GRAPEFRUIT SNOW

MANGO ICE CREAM

LEMON CREAM

APPLE AND BANANA CHIFFON

CUMQUAT AND GINGER COMPÔTE

ORANGE SOUFFLÉ

SUMMER PUDDING

Served hot:

STRAWBERRY SOUFFLÉ WITH LIQUEUR

BRANDIED APPLES

BANANAS IN RUM

SHERRIED QUINCES

SPICED RHUBARB

CLAFOUTIS

BECAUSE MORE OF US today are weight-conscious, we tend to favour a light chilled dessert—or a platter of fresh fruit—rather than the heavy steamed puddings, pies and elaborate cakes that were popular with previous generations. Obviously, the choice of pudding is governed by what comes before it: when the main course is rich and spicy, a fresh, light, fruit-flavoured dessert provides the necessary contrast in taste and texture; if you wish to forget about calories and indulge in a rich, delicious concoction at the end of the meal, then the preceding courses must be kept simple. Most of the following recipes are easy and quick to prepare.

ORANGES ORIENTALES

❧

(This is a specialty of the Caprice restaurant in London)
4 large (or 8 small) oranges
Syrup of 1 pint water, 4 ounces sugar, 1 ounce glucose

To prepare candied peel, peel oranges finely and cut the pieces into thin strips. (Skin them with a potato peeler to obtain all the zest without the bitter pith.) Soak peel for 24 hours in salted water to remove bitterness, wash, and cook for 15 minutes. Drain off syrup, and cook peel in a stronger syrup made with water, sugar and glucose until well-cooked. Remove all remaining white pith from oranges, core and place the whole oranges in a basin. Make another light syrup of water, sugar and orange skin, cook until it reaches the soft boiling stage, then pour over the oranges. Allow to cool for 24 hours. Serve with some of the syrup and top with candied peel. Serves 4.

COEUR À LA CRÈME

❧

1 pound cottage cheese, creamed
1 pound cream cheese
1 cup heavy cream
4 tablespoons honey

Pass cottage cheese through a fine strainer. Mix well with softened cream cheese, cream and honey. Or blend everything in an electric blender until smooth. Pour into a large heart-shaped mould, with holes for drainage, lined with a dampened piece of cheesecloth large enough to fold over the cheese. Close cheesecloth tightly over the mixture, and pack it down with the hands. Place mould on a plate to drain, and chill overnight. At serving time, unmould and serve with fresh strawberries and sweet or sour cream.

RUM SOUR-CREAM MOUSSE

❧

1 bar dark chocolate
1 pint sour cream
½ cup almond macaroons, crumbled
4 ounces granulated sugar
1 tablespoon rum
1 teaspoon vanilla

With a little practice, rum sour-cream mousse can be made in minutes the evening before a party and kept in the refrigerator until serving time. Melt the chocolate, broken in pieces, in a basin over hot water; mix remaining ingredients together thoroughly. Turn into a refrigerator tray and freeze until solid (this will take three hours at least). To serve, unmould on to dish and shave some paler chocolate on top.

FIGS CHANTILLY

※

6 to 8 large ripe green figs
Castor sugar to taste
½ pint cream

1 tablespoon Maraschino
3 tablespoons liqueur

Cut figs down from stalk end in quarters, but do not completely detach them from the base. Sprinkle with Maraschino. Chill. Beat cream with castor sugar to taste, and when it is quite stiff, beat in liqueur; pile into centre of figs.

APRICOT COINTREAU

※

1 pound dried apricots
1 orange (rind and pulp),
   finely shredded
4 ounces granulated sugar

2 to 4 tablespoons Cointreau
½ pint cream, whipped
2 tablespoons almonds,
   blanched and slivered

Simmer apricots, orange rind and pulp gently, uncovered, for 30 minutes. Stir in sugar and continue to cook over very low heat until most of the liquid is absorbed and the apricots are cooked through, adding more water if necessary. Allow apricot mixture to cool and purée it in an electric blender or rub through a fine sieve. Add Cointreau to taste, stir in whipped cream and blanched slivered almonds. Serve in individual dessert dishes.

COFFEE LIQUEUR FOAM

※

½ pint water
4 ounces brown sugar
¼ teaspoon salt
2 heaped teaspoons instant coffee
1 envelope plain gelatine
¼ pint evaporated milk

3 tablespoons Crème de Cacao
   liqueur
2 bananas, sliced
Whipped cream
2 teaspoons Crème de Menthe
   liqueur
Chopped nuts

Heat water with brown sugar, salt and instant coffee. Sprinkle in gelatine, allow to dissolve, then pour into large bowl. Set aside until mixture begins to thicken. Add evaporated milk and Crème de Cacao. Beat until thick and foamy. Add finely-sliced bananas and spoon into stemmed glasses. Chill until set. To serve, top with whipped cream (about 2 teaspoons Crème de Menthe stirred into the whipped cream gives a delicious flavour and will blend perfectly with the coffee). Sprinkle with chopped nuts. Serves 8.

ORANGE SHERBET

⊰❀⊱

1 cup water
1 cup granulated sugar
½ cup lemon juice
4 cups frozen orange juice

½ cup bitter orange marmalade
½ cup Grand Marnier liqueur
2 to 3 tablespoons heavy cream

This should be served softly frozen, not hard. Freezing will take about 2 to 3 hours in ice trays in the refrigerator freezing compartment. Heat water and sugar together until they come to a boil. Add the lemon juice and combine with the thawed orange juice. Fold in marmalade and Grand Marnier and freeze in ice trays. Remove the sherbet when barely frozen, beat well with a fork and return to the freezing compartment. Repeating this process will improve the sherbet, or you may prefer to incorporate some heavy cream, which will give it a smoother texture.

RUM SOUFFLÉ

⊰❀⊱

¼ pint water
¼ pound castor sugar
6 tablespoons rum
4 ounces unsweetened chocolate
¼ pint coffee

2 tablespoons brown sugar
2 ounces butter
4 eggs
Sponge fingers
Whipped cream

Make a syrup by boiling water, sugar and rum together for 3 to 5 minutes. Melt the chocolate in a small saucepan. Add coffee and cook for 5 minutes. Remove saucepan from heat; separate eggs. Add brown sugar, butter and egg yolks, and mix well. Fold in stiffly beaten egg whites. Sprinkle the sponge fingers with the rum syrup and use them to line the moulds. Pour in chocolate mixture. Arrange other sponge fingers on top of the moulds. Chill overnight. Unmould and serve with whipped cream.

MOCHA MARSHMALLOW

⊰❀⊱

1 heaped tablespoon instant coffee
1 cup boiling water

30 large marshmallows
1 cup heavy cream
½ teaspoon vanilla essence

Dissolve coffee in boiling water. Add marshmallows, place over low heat and stir until melted. Add cream; stir well and cool. Flavour with vanilla. Place in small bowl, rinsed in cold water, and chill until set. Serve with cream. Serves 4.

CRÈME PARISIENNE

⊹⊱❈⊰⊹

4 egg yolks
¾ cup granulated sugar
2 teaspoons plain gelatine

½ cup Australian hock or Chablis
½ cup almonds, toasted
1 pint cream, whipped

Beat egg yolks until light and lemon-coloured. Add sugar; continue beating until thoroughly blended. Soak gelatine in cold, dry white wine. Dissolve over boiling water. Slowly pour over it the egg mixture, beating briskly with wire whisk to prevent curdling. Stir in toasted almonds (slivered and sprinkled with a few drops of almond essence). Fold in cream whipped with a few grains of salt. Pour into a mould, previously dipped in cold water, and chill in refrigerator at least 4 hours. Unmould; serve with a sweet sauce.

APRICOT MOUSSE

⊹⊱❈⊰⊹

1 lemon
1 pound dried apricots
8 ounces applesauce

4 egg whites
Almonds

Pare rind of lemon with vegetable peeler; squeeze lemon. Simmer dried apricots which have been soaked in water, the applesauce, lemon juice and rind for 30 minutes uncovered. Drain off excess juice and press mixture through sieve. Cool; add sugar to taste. Whip egg whites stiffly, then put beater in apricot purée. Whip purée, gradually adding egg whites. Heap into serving dish and chill. Garnish with almonds.

SACHER TORTE

⊹⊱❈⊰⊹

2 to 3 cups butter
¾ cup granulated sugar
8 eggs

6 ounces semi-sweet chocolate
Apricot jam

ICING: 2 ounces chocolate, 1 dessertspoon butter, 3 tablespoons hot water.

Cream butter, add ½ cup sugar and beat in egg yolks one by one, then melted chocolate. Beat egg whites with ¼ cup of sugar and fold into the mixture. Pour into a buttered spring-form tin. Bake in preheated oven (350°F.) for 1¼ hours. Cool; cover top with a layer of apricot jam and the sides and top with chocolate icing made by mixing together over low heat until smooth, the chocolate, butter and hot water.

BISCUIT TORTONI

¼ cup boiling water
¾ cup sugar
5 egg yolks
1 tablespoon Cognac

1 teaspoon vanilla essence
½ cup ground almonds, toasted
1 pint cream, whipped
Toasted almonds, slivered

Set refrigerator at coldest point. Boil water and sugar together until syrupy, about 5 minutes. Beat egg yolks in top of double boiler; gradually add the syrup, beating steadily. Place over hot water and stir until thick. Add Cognac and vanilla. Cool. Fold in almonds and cream. Pour into 6 large or 12 small paper cups. Sprinkle with toasted slivered almonds and freeze 3 to 4 hours.

COFFEE SPONGE

2 envelopes plain gelatine
2 rounded tablespoons instant
  coffee
2 cups boiling water

2 to 3 cups granulated sugar
½ cup cold water
3 egg whites

Soak gelatine in cold water for 5 minutes. Dissolve instant coffee in boiling water. Add the soaked gelatine and 2 to 3 cups sugar and stir well over low heat. Cool. Place mixture in refrigerator until it begins to jell, about 40 minutes. Remove from refrigerator. Beat 3 egg whites until stiff. Add to the coffee mixture and beat with a rotary beater for 5 minutes until light and foamy. Place in a 2-quart mould, rinsed in cold water. Refrigerate until set, about 2 hours. Run a knife around the edge and dip for a second or two in hot water. Turn out on to dish. Serve with cream. Serves 6.

PEACHES STUFFED WITH MACAROONS

2 tablespoons sugar
½ cup water
Lemon juice

4 peaches, stoned and split
4 coconut macaroons
2 tablespoons brandy

Put the sugar, water and lemon juice in a saucepan and dissolve sugar. Pour syrup over halved peaches. Crush macaroons and mix with brandy. Fill peach centres with macaroon mixture and place in a shallow casserole, surrounded by the sugar syrup. Cover and cook for 10 to 15 minutes in oven (300°F.) Cool and serve with chocolate ice cream and sponge lady-fingers.

GRAPEFRUIT SNOW

❧✿❧

3 large grapefruit
4 tablespoons Grenadine
1 envelope plain gelatine
¼ cup cold water

½ cup granulated sugar
½ cup boiling water
2 egg whites

Cut grapefruits in half crosswise. Squeeze and strain juice from four of the halves (should make 1½ cups). With a teaspoon scoop out the sections and discard any seeds from the two remaining halves. Pour Grenadine over the fruit sections and chill. Soak gelatine in cold water for 5 minutes. Moisten sugar in boiling water and boil 1 minute; add gelatine and stir well. Add the 1½ cups grapefruit juice and stir well. Place in two refrigerator freezing trays, turn the control to coldest, and freeze until mushy, about 30 to 45 minutes, depending on your refrigerator. Scrape into a bowl. Beat egg whites until stiff and fold into the partially-frozen sherbet. Beat with rotary beater for 5 minutes and place in a deep round 1½-quart mould. Return to freezing compartment until stiff, about 2 hours. To serve, run a knife around the edge and turn out carefully into a deep dish. Garnish with the chilled bright pink grapefruit sections. Serves 4.

MANGO ICE CREAM

❧✿❧

2 cups mango pulp
1 lemon
¾ cup granulated sugar
2 eggs

2 tablespoons granulated sugar
½ teaspoon almond extract
1 cup heavy cream

Peel 1 or 2 soft, ripe mangoes and cut pulp away from pith. Mash with potato masher to give 2 cups mashed pulp. Add strained lemon juice and ¾ cup sugar. Mix well. Place in shallow ice tray in refrigerator freezing compartment and freeze for about 1 hour. Separate eggs and beat whites with 2 tablespoons sugar until stiff. With the same beater, beat yolks until light and fold them into the whites. With another beater, beat cream until it is as thick as custard but not stiff, and fold into egg mixture. Scrape frozen pulp into a bowl. Add cream and egg mixture and almond extract. Mix lightly but thoroughly, place mixture in container and freeze until stiff, stirring once or twice during the freezing process. In about 2½ hours the cream should be ready. Serves 6.

LEMON CREAM

✦

3 eggs, separated
1 cup granulated sugar
1 envelope plain gelatine
½ cup cold water
Juice of 2 lemons

Juice of 1 small orange
1 teaspoon lemon rind, grated
1 teaspoon orange rind, grated
1 cup cream, whipped

Beat egg yolks and sugar until thick and lemon coloured. Soften gelatine in cold water, dissolve over hot water and stir into egg mixture. Add lemon and orange juices, grated lemon and orange rinds. Mix well. Chill until mixture begins to thicken. Beat egg whites until stiff; fold in whipped cream and then egg whites. Chill until set.

APPLE AND BANANA CHIFFON

✦

1 envelope gelatine
3 tablespoons water
2 eggs
3 tablespoons sugar
2 medium-sized ripe bananas

Thick applesauce
½ teaspoon vanilla essence
1 tablespoon sour cream
Nutmeg

Soak the gelatine in 3 tablespoons cold water in a small saucepan; dissolve over low heat, and cool. Beat eggs and sugar with an electric mixer at high speed for 10 minutes, or until thick and light. Meanwhile, mash bananas and add enough applesauce to make 1½ cups altogether. Stir in vanilla, sour cream and gelatine. Fold in egg and sugar mixture. Pour into 4 bowls. Sprinkle with nutmeg. Chill until set.

CUMQUAT AND GINGER COMPÔTE

✦

6 canned pears, halved
9 pieces of preserved ginger
Syrup from cumquats

12-ounce can preserved cumquats
Juice from canned pears
4 tablespoons brown sugar

Arrange the pears, placing cumquats on top of each pear, in an ovenproof serving dish. Sliver the ginger and scatter all over. Combine juice, syrup and sugar, pour over the fruit and bake in preheated oven (350°F.) for 40 minutes. Chill; serve with ice cream and decorate with slivered almonds.

ORANGE SOUFFLÉ

◦⊰❄⊱◦

4 eggs
3 egg yolks
6 tablespoons granulated sugar
1½ tablespoons plain gelatine
2 teaspoons lemon juice

3 tablespoons water
1 large orange
2 cups cream, whipped
Red currant jelly

Put eggs, egg yolks and sugar in bowl; beat with electric mixer until thick. Dissolve gelatine in lemon juice and water over low heat. Carefully stir this into egg mousse, with grated rind and juice of the orange. Mix in whipped cream. Tie a band of greaseproof paper around an 8-inch soufflé dish. Pour in mixture and set in refrigerator for about 2 hours. Remove and arrange around the edge skinned sections of another orange. Dip a soft brush into red currant jelly and carefully cover top of the soufflé with jelly. Chill again and remove paper collar before serving. Serves 8 to 10.

SUMMER PUDDING

◦⊰❄⊱◦

½ pound apples
1 pound raspberries or
   blackcurrants

½ pound granulated sugar
White bread, sliced

Peel and core apples. Add them to the raspberries or blackcurrants with sugar. Heat gently until sugar dissolves and juice leaves the fruit. Butter inside of a pudding basin and line with slices of stale white bread from which the crusts have been cut. Fill this with fruit and top with bread. Butter bottom of a small plate that will fit into the top of the basin. Place on top of pudding and put a weight on top of this. Leave overnight in a cool place. Unmould and serve with cream.

STRAWBERRY SOUFFLÉ WITH LIQUEUR

◦⊰❄⊱◦

1 punnet ripe firm strawberries
1 cup granulated sugar
¼ cup Kirsch

10 egg whites
Whipped cream

Hull the strawberries. Sprinkle with 2 tablespoons sugar and Kirsch. Let stand for 1 hour. Caramelise ½ cup sugar and line a soufflé dish with the caramel. Beat egg whites stiffly; add remaining sugar very gradually. Fold in drained strawberries and pour into casserole dish. Stand in a pan of hot water and place in preheated oven (375°F.). Bake until puffy and lightly browned. Serve at once with whipped cream, delicately flavoured with Kirsch and sugar to taste.

BRANDIED APPLES

6 cooking apples
6 ounces sultanas or raisins
2 ounces butter
Cinnamon
1 cup of white wine
1 tablespoon of water

Slices of lemon peel
2 tablespoons brandy
½ cup marmalade
2 teaspoons cornflour
2 tablespoons brown sugar

Wash and core apples, spoon out the centres. Pierce apples with a fork to prevent skins breaking. Stuff with sultanas or raisins, dot with butter, and dust with cinnamon and sugar. Mix the wine, water and lemon peel and pour over apples in a shallow casserole dish. Bake (350°F.) for about 40 minutes or until they can be pierced with a skewer. Remove apples to a serving dish and stir liquid until it boils. Add the brandy. Stir in marmalade and cornflour. Pour 3 tablespoons of sauce over each apple and glaze in a hot oven for a few minutes. Serve with ice cream.

BANANAS IN RUM

2 tablespoons brown sugar
½ cup water
6 firm bananas
Lemon juice
2 tablespoons rum

Cinnamon
Grated lemon rind
1 ounce almonds, shelled and
 blanched

Put sugar and water in saucepan and dissolve sugar. Peel bananas and coat with lemon juice. Place in shallow casserole dish with sugar liquid and rum. Dust with cinnamon and grated lemon rind. Cover and cook in oven (300°F.) for 15 to 20 minutes. Serve with mocha ice cream and decorate with slivered almonds.

SHERRIED QUINCES

3 tablespoons liquid honey
1 cup water
4 large quinces

2 ounces crystallised ginger
4 teaspoons sweet sherry
Chopped nuts

Bring honey and water to boil. Peel and core quinces; place in casserole. Cover with the sliced ginger, add sherry and honey. Cover with tightly-fitting lid and cook in the top shelf of oven (250°F.) for about 2 hours. Serve with cream or ice cream sprinkled with chopped nuts.

SPICED RHUBARB

❖

2 ounces sultanas
2 ounces raisins
2 ounces currants
1 pound rhubarb
1 teaspoon mixed spices

1 teaspoon ground cinnamon
$\frac{1}{4}$ cup brown sugar
$\frac{1}{2}$ cup apricot juice
1 cup Sauterne

Grease a shallow casserole. Clean dried fruit. Wipe rhubarb, cut into $\frac{1}{2}$-inch pieces and mix with dried fruit and spices. Melt brown sugar in fruit juice, add Sauterne and pour over the mixture of rhubarb. Cover closely and bake in a slow oven (270°F.) about 30 to 35 minutes. Cook slowly to prevent rhubarb from becoming stringy. Serve with ice cream.

CLAFOUTIS

❖

2 cups fresh, dark cherries
2 tablespoons butter
$\frac{1}{2}$ cup castor sugar
$1\frac{1}{2}$ cups milk

2 eggs
6 tablespoons flour
$\frac{1}{2}$ pint cream

Preheat oven (400°F.). Wash, stem and pit the cherries. Butter a $9\frac{1}{2}$-inch ovenproof glass pie plate with 1 tablespoon butter. Sprinkle the cherries with $\frac{1}{4}$ cup of castor sugar, mix and spread over the pie plate. Make a smooth batter of the milk, eggs, 1 tablespoon of melted butter, flour and remaining $\frac{1}{4}$ cup of castor sugar. If you use an electric blender, place the ingredients in the glass container in the order given and run at low speed while you count 20. Pour over the cherries. Bake about 30 minutes, reducing the heat (325°F.) for the last 10 minutes if necessary to prevent over-crisping. Serve at once, sprinkled with castor sugar and accompanied by cream.

Late Night Suppers

BEEF STROGANOFF

DUCK LIVERS AND RICE

SNOB WELSH RAREBIT

CHEESE FONDUE

CRABMEAT IN SKILLET

OEUFS VAUDOISES

CROQUE MONSIEUR

CHICKEN LIVERS AND MUSHROOMS

MACARONI CHEESE

CHEESE AND GUINNESS FONDUE

COLD KEDGEREE

FRENCH HAM AND EGG RING

PRAWNS ONDINE

POTTED SHRIMPS

An evening's entertainment planned around taking a party to the theatre raises the question of when (and what) to feed the guests. To dine before you go may mean hastily served food consumed at a barbarously early hour, with the host surreptitiously consulting his watch between courses. Or else the sense of urgency dissipates as the dinner progresses, with the result that you miss half the first act! A more relaxed arrangement is to invite guests home *after* the show for a late supper. This may be cold food prepared in advance, a reheated casserole, or a quick chafing-dish production at the table.

BEEF STROGANOFF
(cooked in a chafing-dish)

✦❈✦

2 pounds beef fillet
Salt
Freshly-ground black pepper
1 cup sour cream
¼ cup butter
1 onion, quartered and thinly sliced

1 tablespoon flour
1 cup hot beef stock
Pinch of dry mustard
Fresh dill, chopped or
  ½ teaspoon dried dill

Before leaving for theatre, cut beef into strips, 2 inches long, ½ inch wide, ¼ inch thick, and sprinkle with salt and pepper. Do not refrigerate. Let sour cream come to room temperature. At table, heat butter in chafing-dish over direct heat. Brown steak lightly, a few strips at a time, removing browned strips to a warmed bowl. Add onion to pan, cook until soft. Sprinkle with flour, stir in hot stock and cook until sauce bubbles and thickens. Add mustard, dill, browned meat and sour cream, and mix. Season to taste. Cover and place chafing-dish in hot water pan over heat. Warm up gently about 15 minutes but do not let sauce boil. It should be light, smooth and a deep amber colour. Serve with rice. Serves 6.

DUCK LIVERS AND RICE
(Mr George Molnar)

✦❈✦

1 pound duck livers
2 onions, chopped
Butter

Chicken fat
Rice

Trim livers. Sauté onion in butter until golden. Melt some chicken fat in separate pan and fry the duck livers in it gently about 5 minutes (they should still be slightly pink inside). Cook rice, add to onions, then add livers. Mix and serve hot with a green salad.

SNOB WELSH RAREBIT

✦❈✦

1 cup beer
½ pound strong Cheddar, grated
1 dessertspoon finely-chopped
  fresh sage, or ½ teaspoon dried sage

½ teaspoon English mustard
Salt and pepper to taste

This quick snack can be prepared when you get home. Warm beer in saucepan, gradually add cheese and other ingredients. Stir until cheese has melted; serve on hot buttered toast triangles.

CHEESE FONDUE

⬧⧉⬧

(This traditional Swiss après ski dish is eaten by everyone dipping into the same pot, so more than four people may be a crowd)

1 pound Swiss cheese, coarsely-grated	3 dessertspoons Kirsch or Cognac
1 clove garlic	White pepper
2 cups dry white wine	Grated nutmeg
1 teaspoon cornflour	French bread

Grate cheese in advance (equal quantities of Emmenthaler and Gruyère are a good mixture). Rub heavy pan with cut garlic clove and heat the wine in it. Meanwhile dissolve cornflour in Kirsch. When wine is almost boiling, add cheese gradually, stirring all the time. Keep heat high but do not let fondue boil. Add cheese until you feel a slight 'pull' on the stirring spoon. Now, stirring constantly, add Kirsch and cornflour mixture. Continue to stir until fondue thickens; transfer to chafing-dish at table (or you can make it in the chafing-dish from the beginning). Add a dash of pepper and sprinkling of nutmeg. Provide crusty French bread cut into bite-sized pieces and let guests take turns to dip their bread in the pot, with a stirring motion of their forks. Keep fondue bubbling.

CRABMEAT IN SKILLET

⬧⧉⬧

2 tablespoons butter	Cognac
½ lemon	Paprika
1 pound crabmeat, cooked	Buttered toast
Salt and pepper	

Heat butter and lemon juice in a skillet, add cooked crabmeat. Season with salt and pepper. Shake skillet constantly so that flavours mingle. When crabmeat is hot, flame it with Cognac if you wish, then dust with paprika and serve on pieces of buttered toast. Serves 4.

OEUFS VAUDOISES

⬧⧉⬧

This is a glamorised version of scrambled eggs, but just as quick and easy to prepare. Make the required quantity of scrambled eggs, using dry vermouth instead of the usual small amount of milk. At the last moment add some peeled prawns, 8 or 10 per person, and top with shaved almonds.

CROQUE MONSIEUR

꧁❀꧂

Grate imported Gruyère cheese (about ⅓ pound for 6 to 8 people) beforehand; if it is rather stale, the grating is easier. Cut thin slices of cooked ham in rounds and soak them in white wine. On your return from the theatre, sandwich each ham slice between rounds of fried bread or buttered toast and arrange side by side in a shallow ovenproof dish. Make a creamy béchamel sauce, add about two-thirds of the grated cheese and stir until sauce is smooth. Pour over sandwiches; sprinkle remaining cheese on top. Place under a hot grill for a few minutes until cheese bubbles and browns. Serve hot: one sandwich apiece should be ample, as the sauce is rich.

CHICKEN LIVERS AND MUSHROOMS
(cooked in a chafing-dish)

꧁❀꧂

3 slices bacon
1 small onion, finely chopped
½ pound chicken livers
¼ pound mushrooms, sliced

Dry white wine
Salt and pepper
Dash of Tabasco sauce
Hot buttered rice

In the kitchen, sauté bacon until crisp, then crumble. At the table, sauté onion in bacon drippings until golden. Add quartered chicken livers, sauté about 5 minutes and then add mushrooms. Sauté another minute or so, then add a little wine, seasoning and Tabasco. Cover and simmer about 5 minutes. Serve on rice with crumbled bacon sprinkled on top.

MACARONI CHEESE

꧁❀꧂

2 cups (8 ounces) elbow
   macaroni
3 tablespoons butter
¼ cup onion, chopped
3 tablespoons flour

Salt and pepper to taste
1 cup cream
½ cup dry white wine
2 cups (about 8 ounces) Cheddar
   cheese, grated

Cook macaroni, drain and put aside. Heat butter and sauté onion until tender. Stir in flour, salt and pepper. Slowly add cream and wine and cook over low heat, stirring constantly, until sauce has thickened. Add cheese and stir until melted. Mix the macaroni and cheese sauce. Transfer to greased 1½-quart casserole. Bake in a preheated oven (350°F.) for 15 minutes. The dish can be reheated in oven after your return from the theatre.

CHEESE AND GUINNESS FONDUE

·❈·

2 pounds Cheddar cheese, grated
½ pint Guinness
6 to 8 tablespoons Worcestershire
  sauce

Salt and pepper
Dash of cayenne
1 tablespoon cornflour

Put grated cheese into a 7-inch fondue dish (or enamelled iron casserole) and melt slowly, stirring continuously. Add rest of ingredients and stir until fondue has thickened slightly. Serve chunks of French bread or toasted white bread for dipping.

COLD KEDGEREE

(Mrs H. G. Scotter)

·❈·

4 ounces long-grain rice
1 smoked haddock
Milk and butter
Pepper
3 hard-boiled eggs
½ pint small cooked prawns

10 anchovy fillets
1 dessertspoon finely-chopped
  parsley
Juice of 1 lemon
Grated lemon rind
½ pint cream

Cook rice, allow to dry out and cool. Poach haddock in milk with a large piece of butter; season with pepper. Flake fish, add to rice. Chop eggs roughly and add to rice mixture with prawns, 4 anchovy fillets, parsley, lemon juice and a pinch of grated rind. Gently mix together, add cream and mix again. Garnish with some more anchovy fillets. Serves 6.

FRENCH HAM AND EGG RING

·❈·

6 eggs
2½ cups ham, chopped
Salt and pepper

8 eggs
Mushrooms
Hollandaise sauce

Butter a ring mould well and carefully break 6 eggs in the bottom so that yolks are unbroken. Cover with ham and season lightly. Add 8 more eggs to top and season again. Cover top of mould with foil and stand in pan of water. Bake (350°F.) for 30 minutes or until eggs are set. Unmould on a platter and fill centre with grilled or sautéed mushrooms. Serve with hollandaise sauce (made earlier and reheated). Serves 6 to 8.

PRAWNS ONDINE

(This dish can be prepared the day before and is served cold)

2 8-ounce cans red salmon
4 tablespoons butter
1 cup cream, whipped
2 cups small cooked prawns
¾ cup mayonnaise

1 tablespoon gelatine
3 tablespoons water
¾ cup white wine
Finely-chopped parsley

Drain salmon and mash. Cream butter, add salmon gradually; beat until light and fluffy. Fold in whipped cream. Line 6 shells or small individual dishes with some of salmon mixture, reserving enough for a cover. Chop prawns and mix with mayonnaise. Fill into prepared dishes and cover with remainder of salmon mixture. Place in freezing compartment of refrigerator. Soften gelatine in water for 5 minutes. Place over hot water until gelatine dissolves. Stir in wine. Spoon over top of salmon and chill until firm. Garnish each dish with a prawn and some parsley. Serves 6.

POTTED SHRIMPS

(Mrs John McCallum)

1 pound cooked baby prawns
3 ounces clarified butter (ghee)
Freshly-ground black pepper

1 teaspoon powdered mace
1 teaspoon paprika

Peel prawns and lightly sauté in butter, adding a grind of black pepper, the mace and paprika. Transfer to a deep pâté dish and top with clarified butter so that it covers the prawns. Refrigerate until set and chilled. Serve with triangles of hot buttered toast as a snack with drinks.

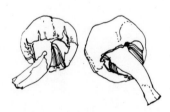

Index

❖